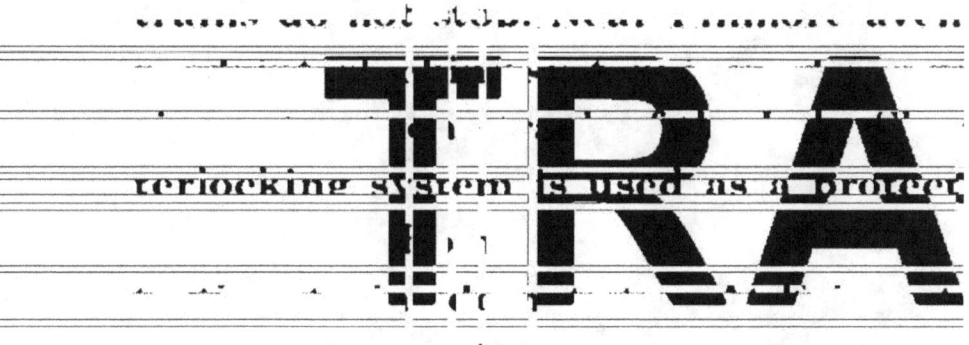

ISBN: 978-0-359-29607-1

Faint Press / Worthington, Ohio, USA / 2018
faintpress.tumblr.com

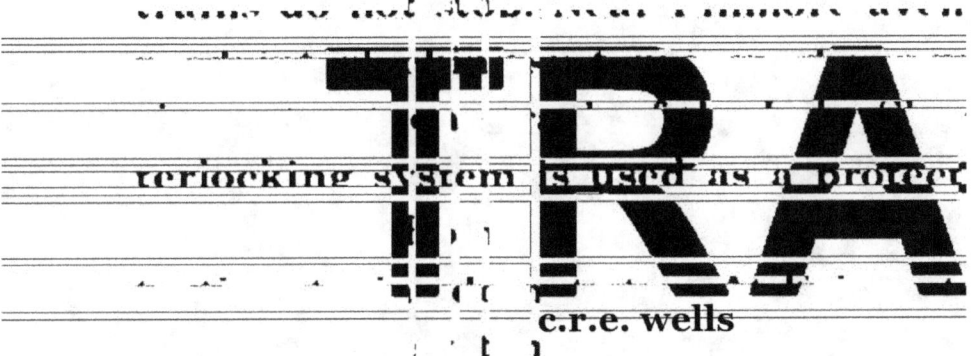

c.r.e. wells

We often blush for the railroad sign painter and sometimes take a shy at him; but he replies that the business of the English language is "to git there," and goes on unabashed.

—Editor, *The Railroad Gazette*, October 7, 1892.

DO NOT

ST P

N

TRACKS

ACKS

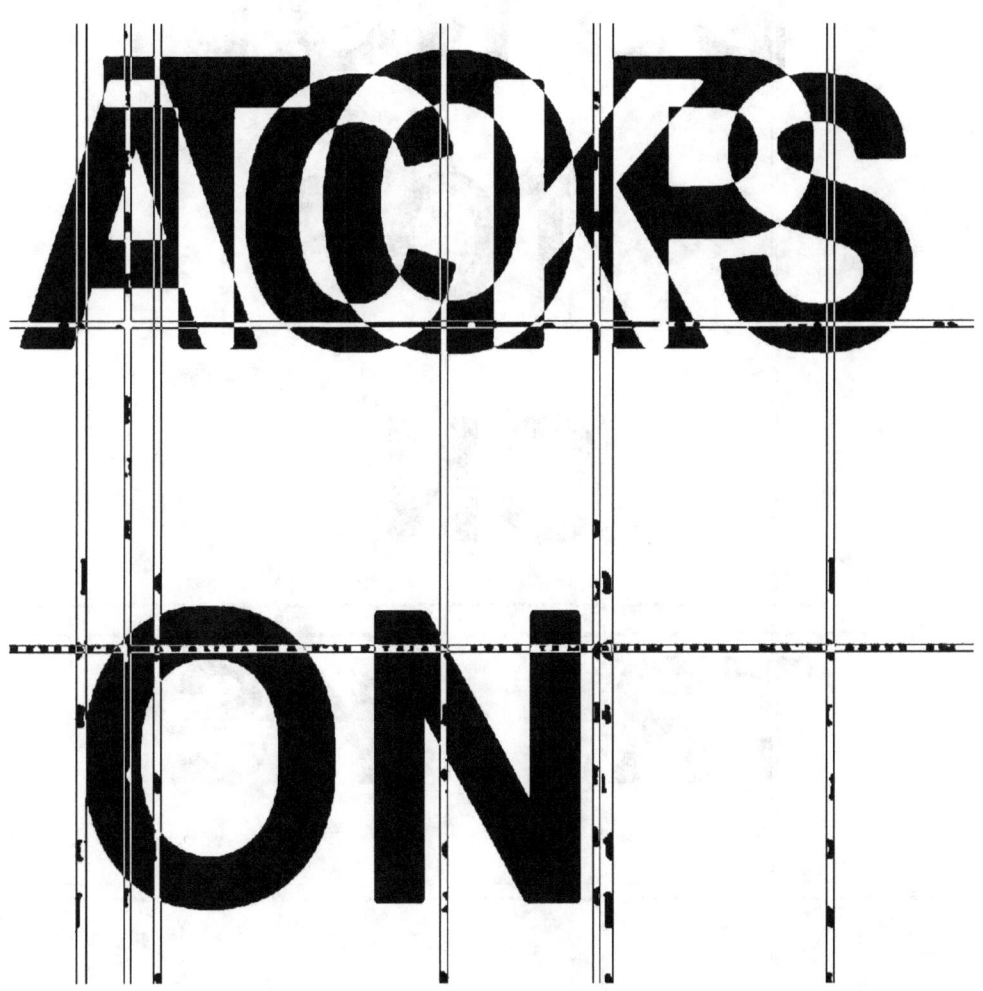

DO NOT
TOP
ON
TR KS

TWO TRACKS OF TRO LORIGH WITHOUT INTERLOCKING SYSTEM IS NOT ON A PROTECTION

O NO

TOP

ON

T CKS

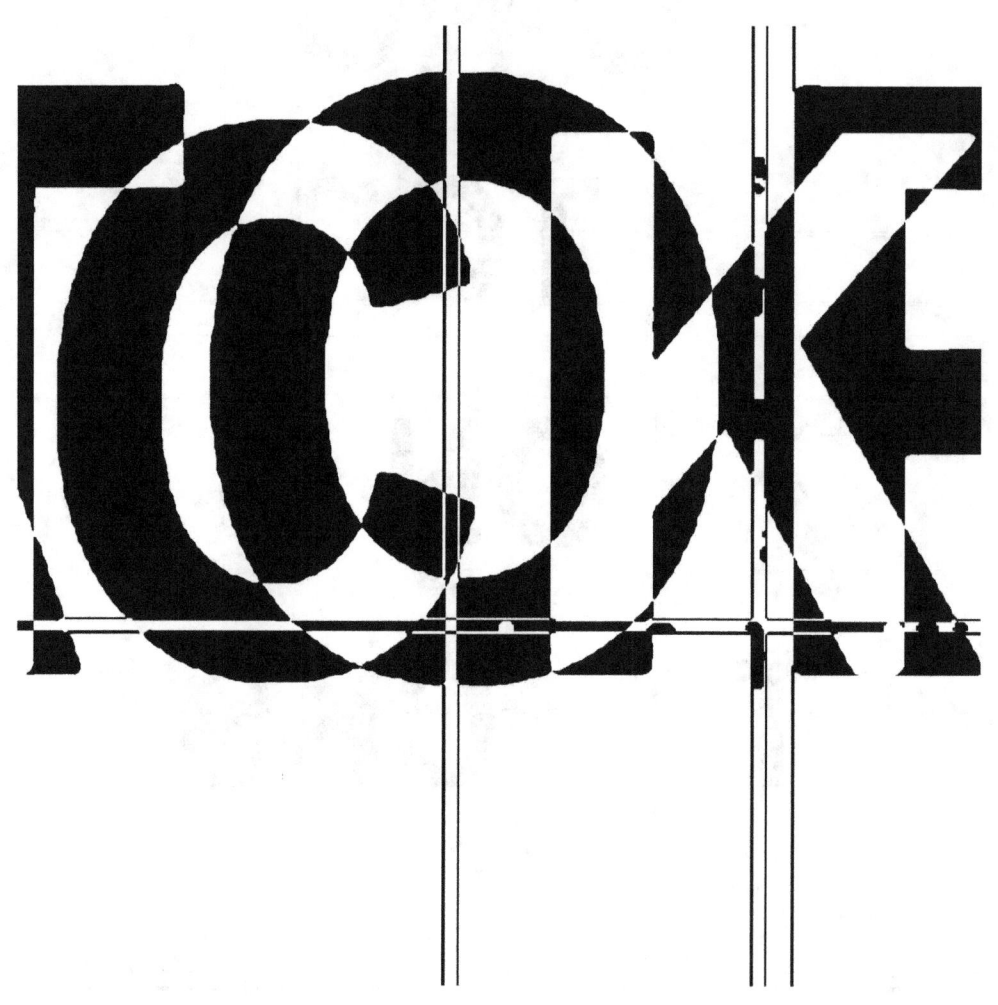

TOP
ON

TOPO
ONON

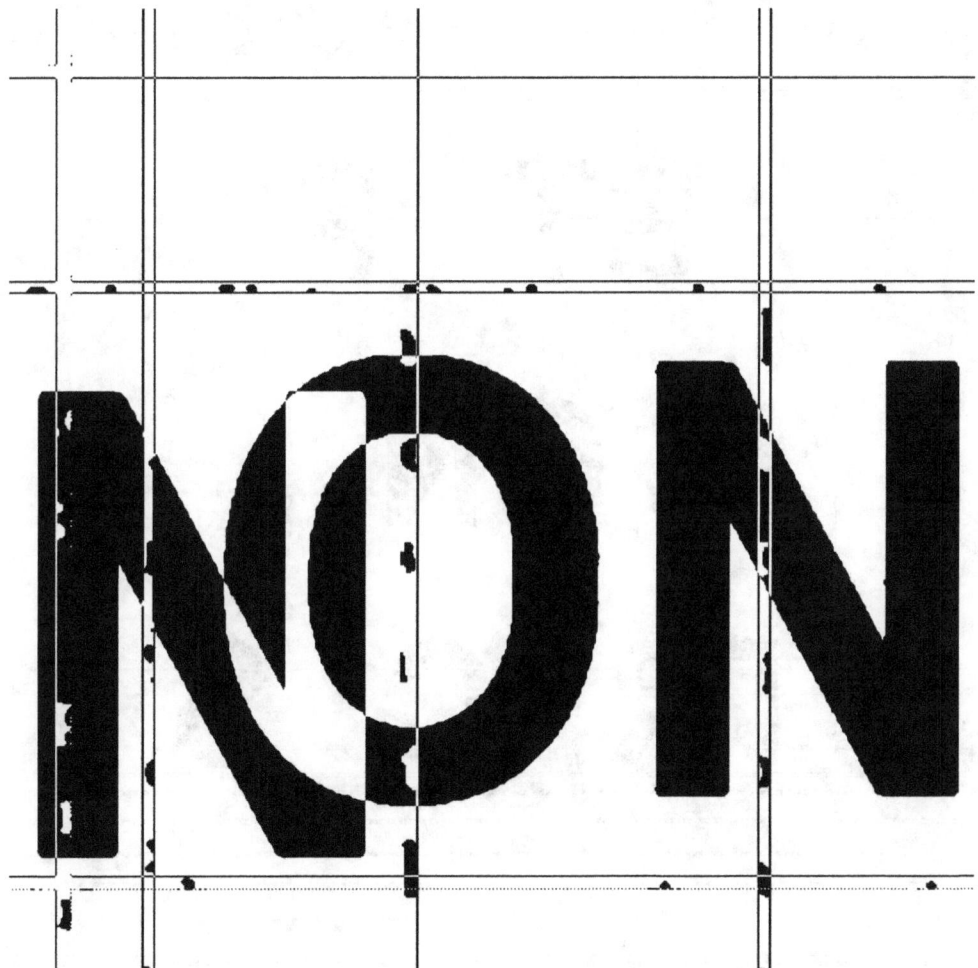

D OT

ST P

ON

TR C S

DO NOT
TO
N
TR CKS

tection trains do not stop. At Fairport, one track of the West Shore Railroad.

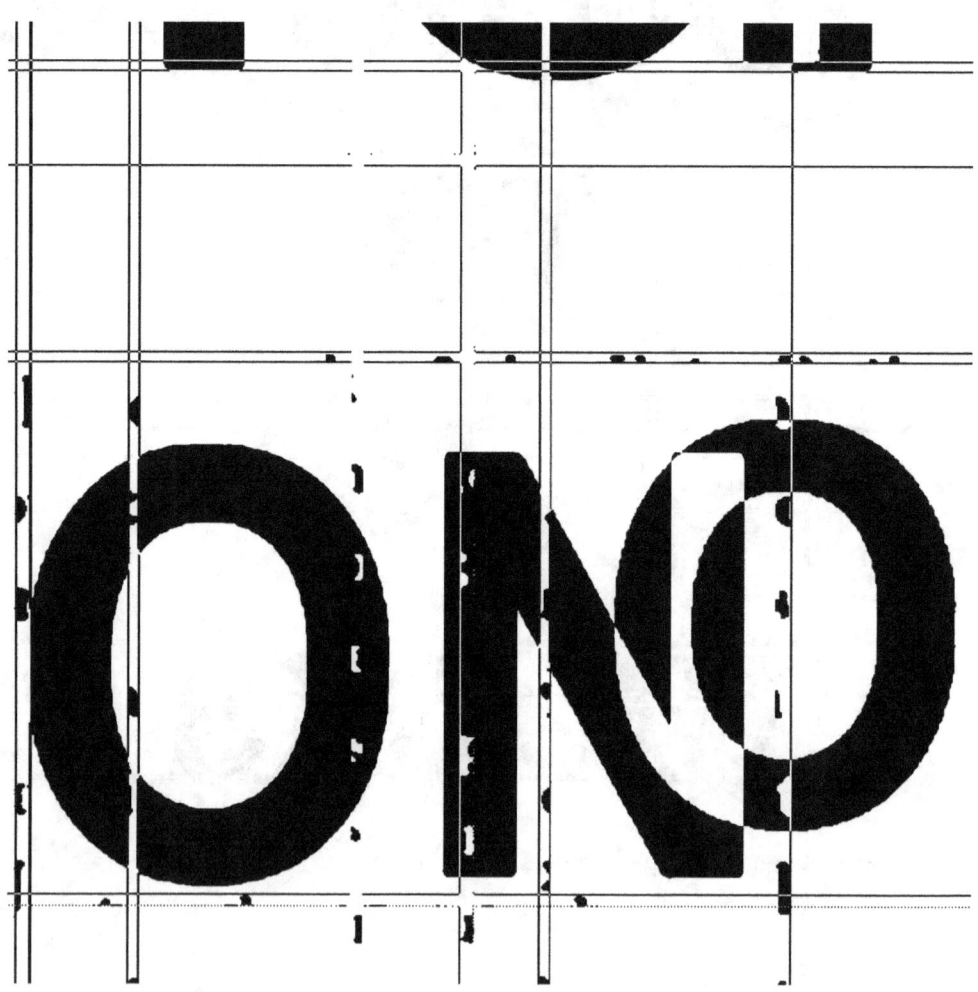

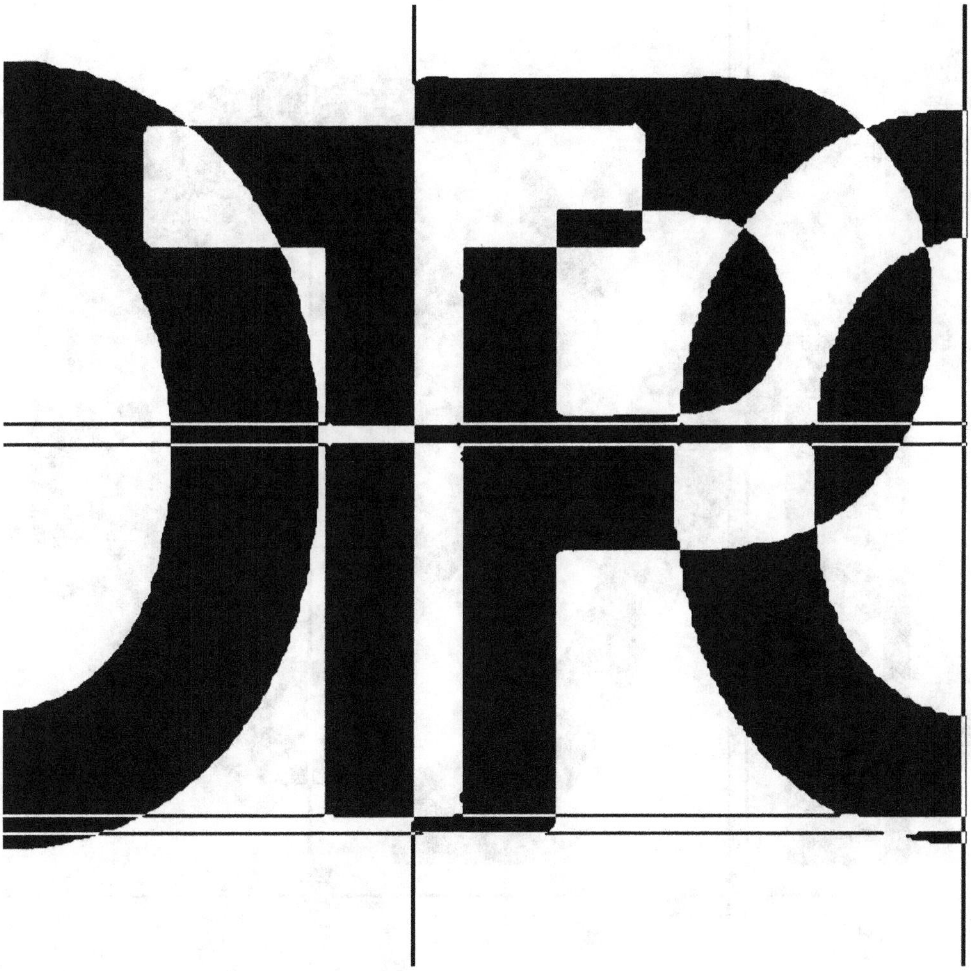

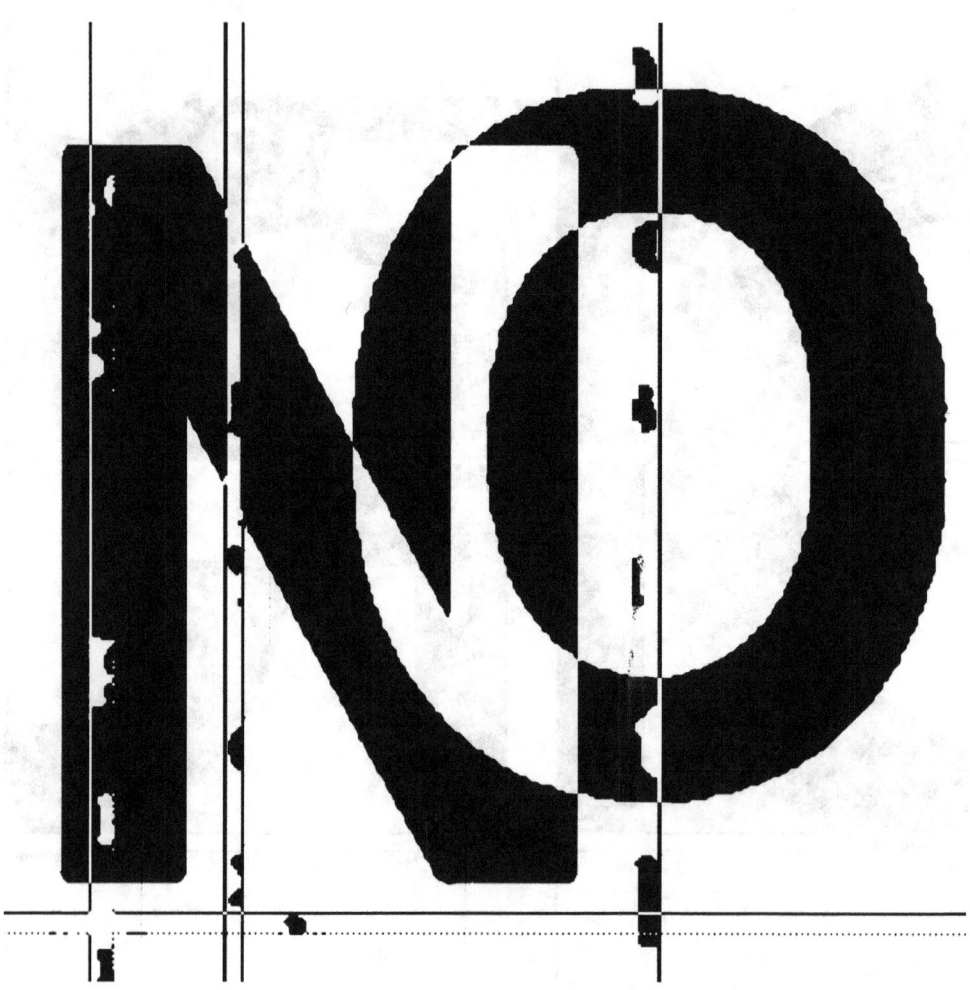

TO
ON

T

STOP

O

RACKS

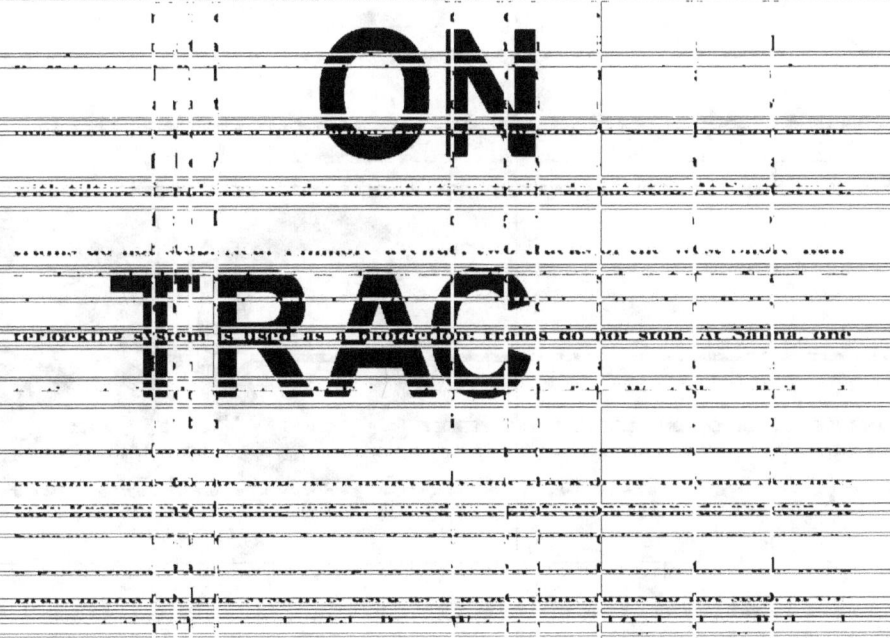

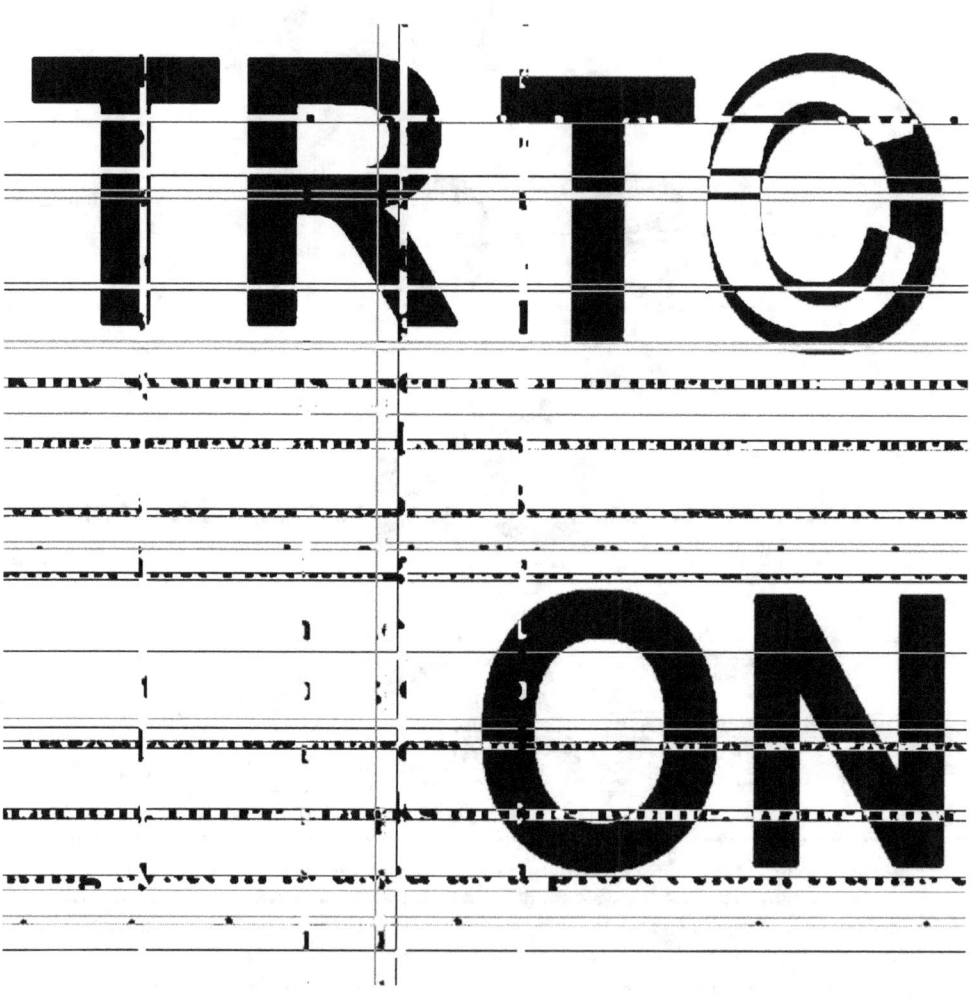

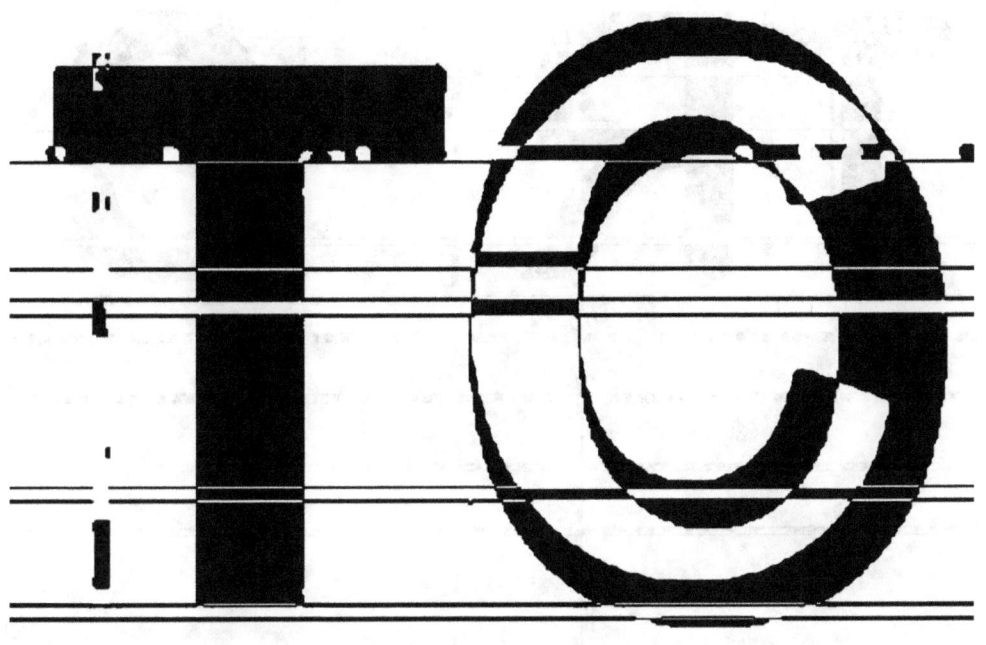

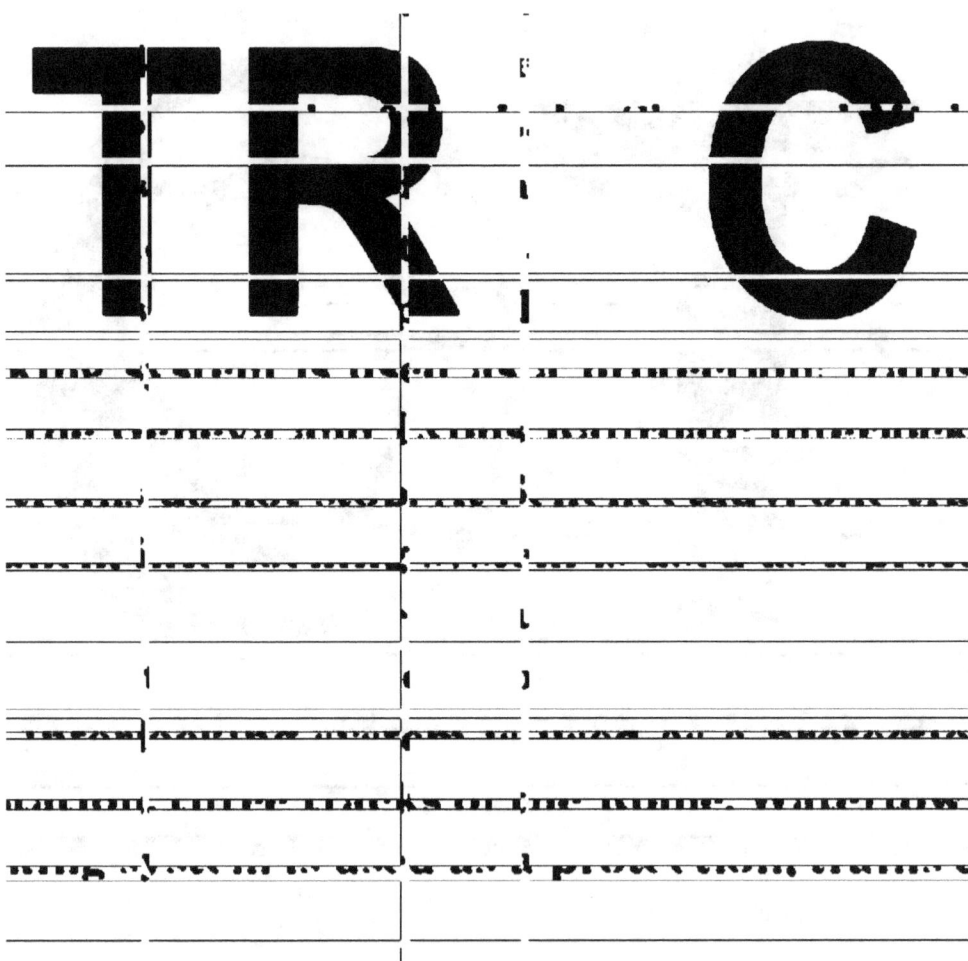

DO NO

TO

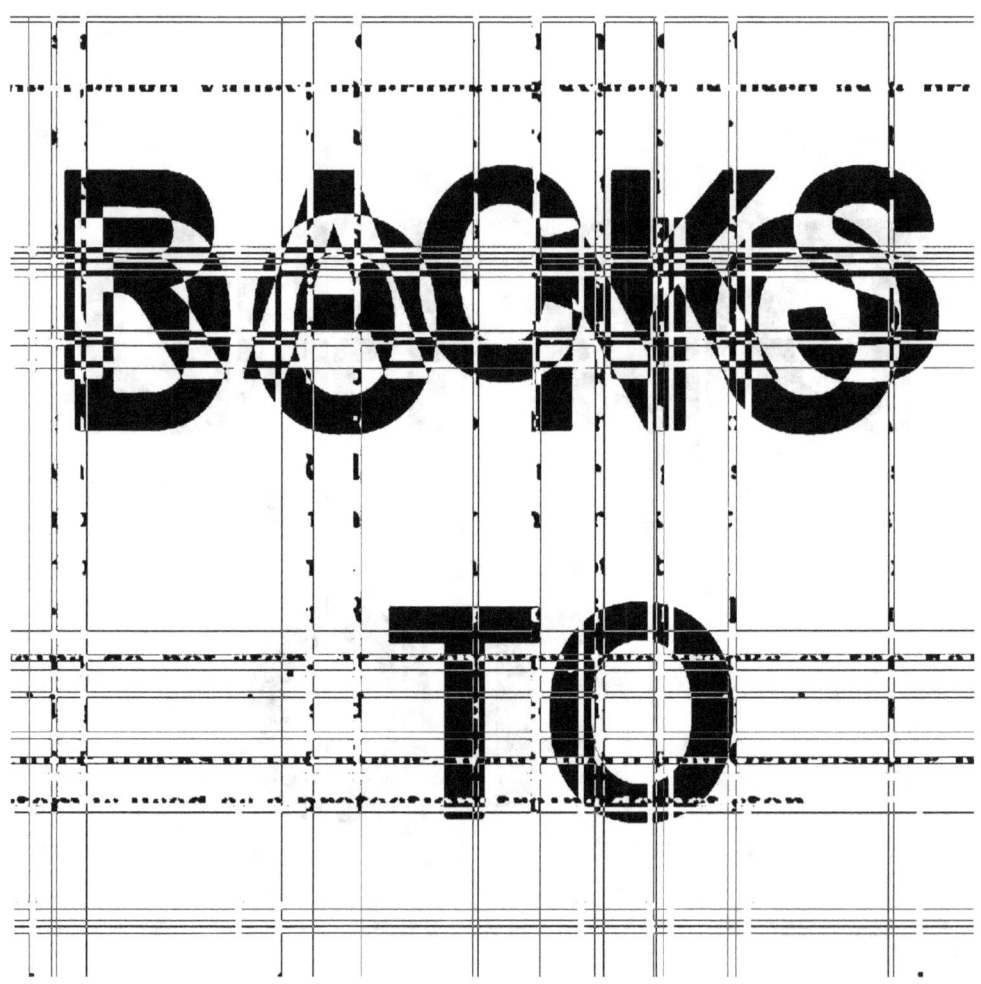

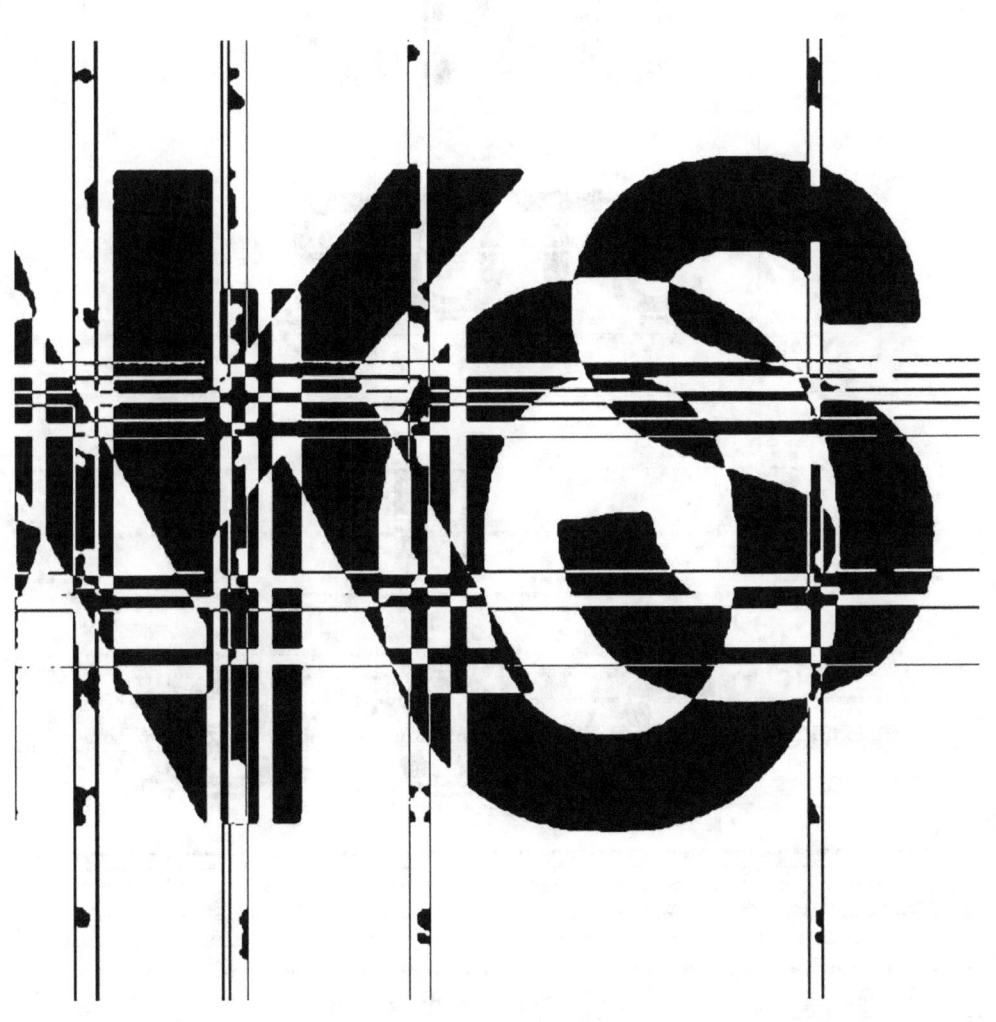

O NO

STOP

N

R C S

O NOT

P

TRACKS

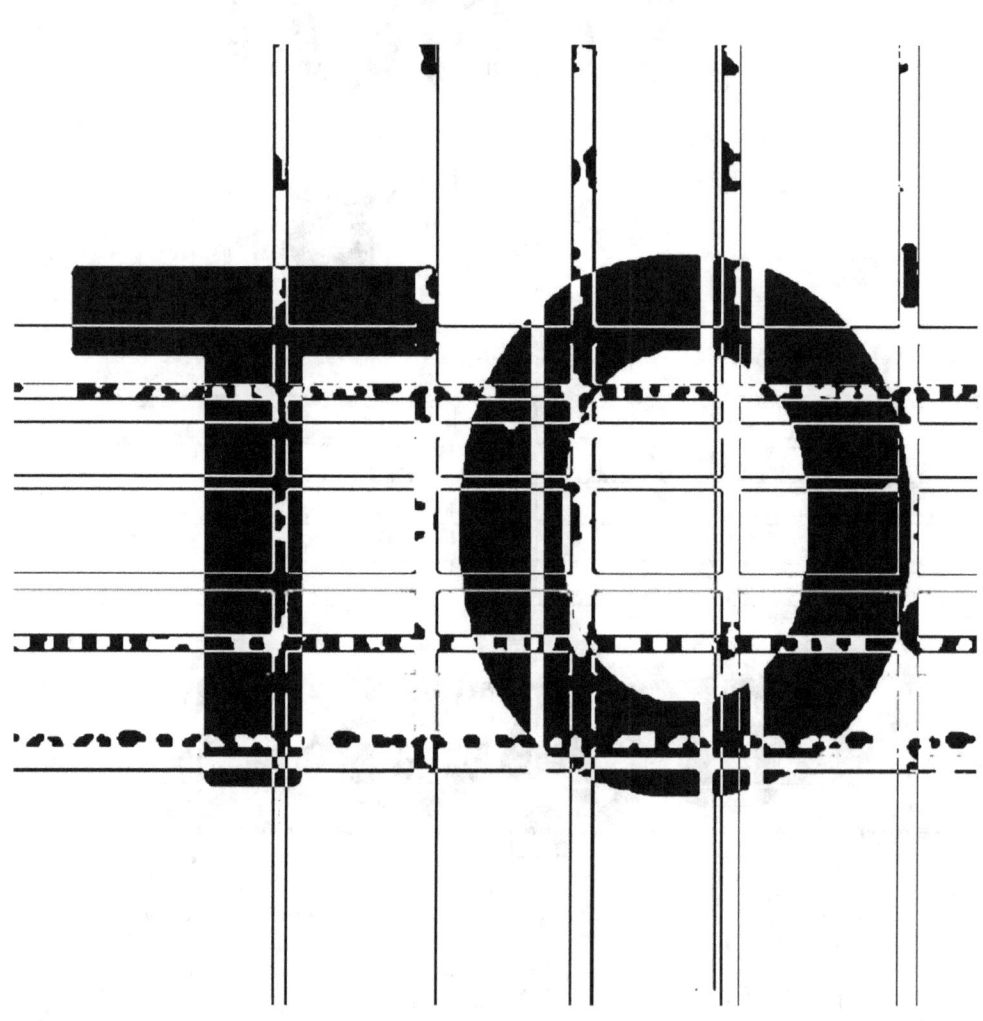

NOT
S O

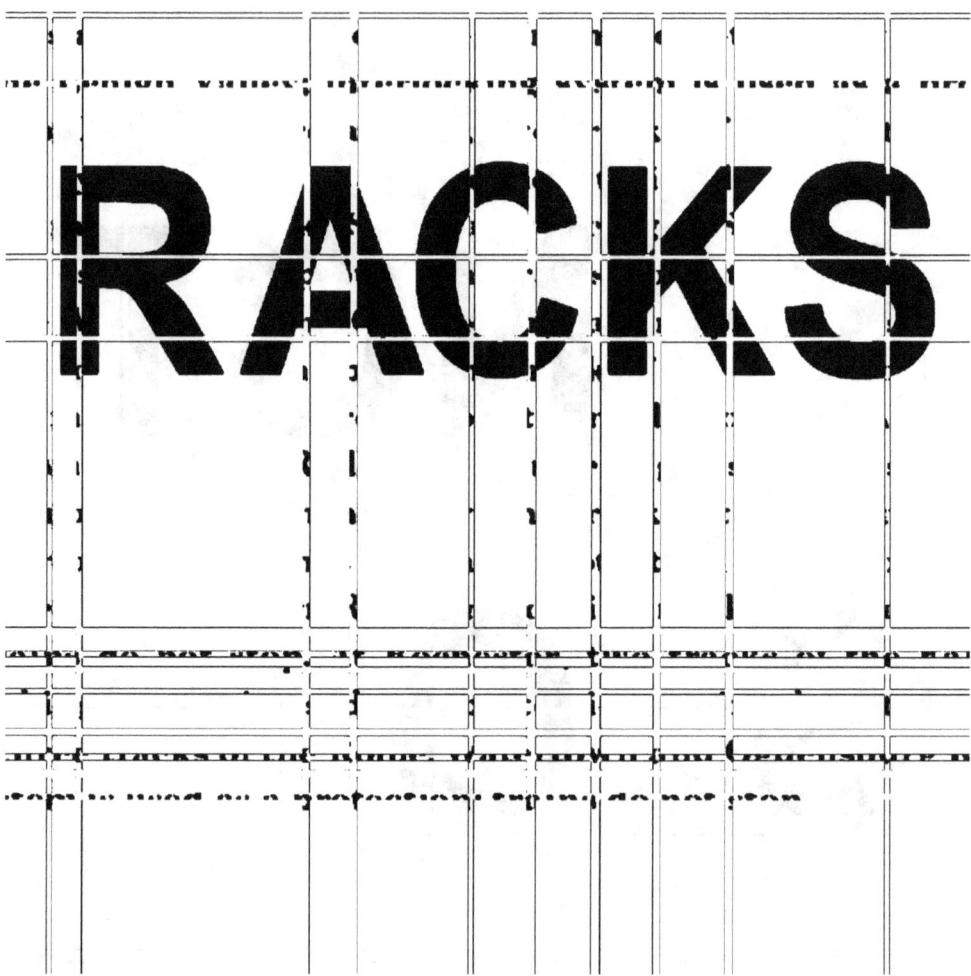

O NOT STOP

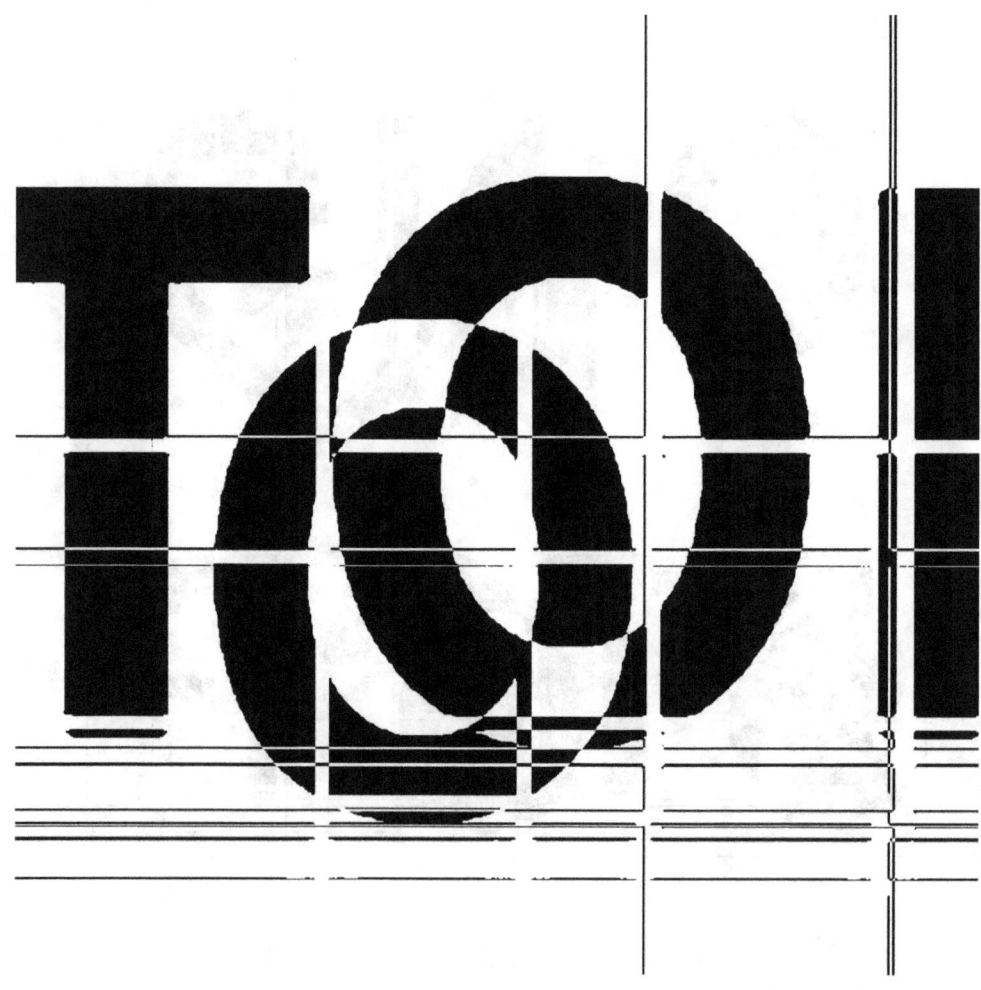

O NO
STOP

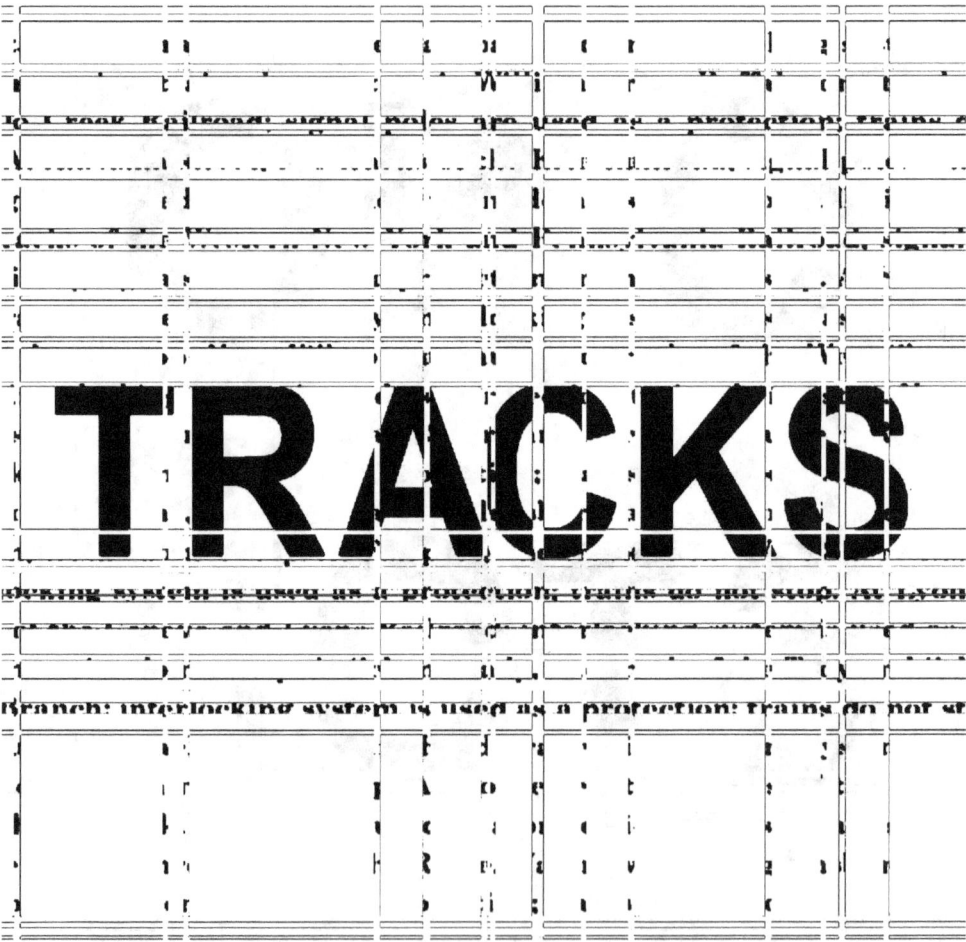

TRACKS

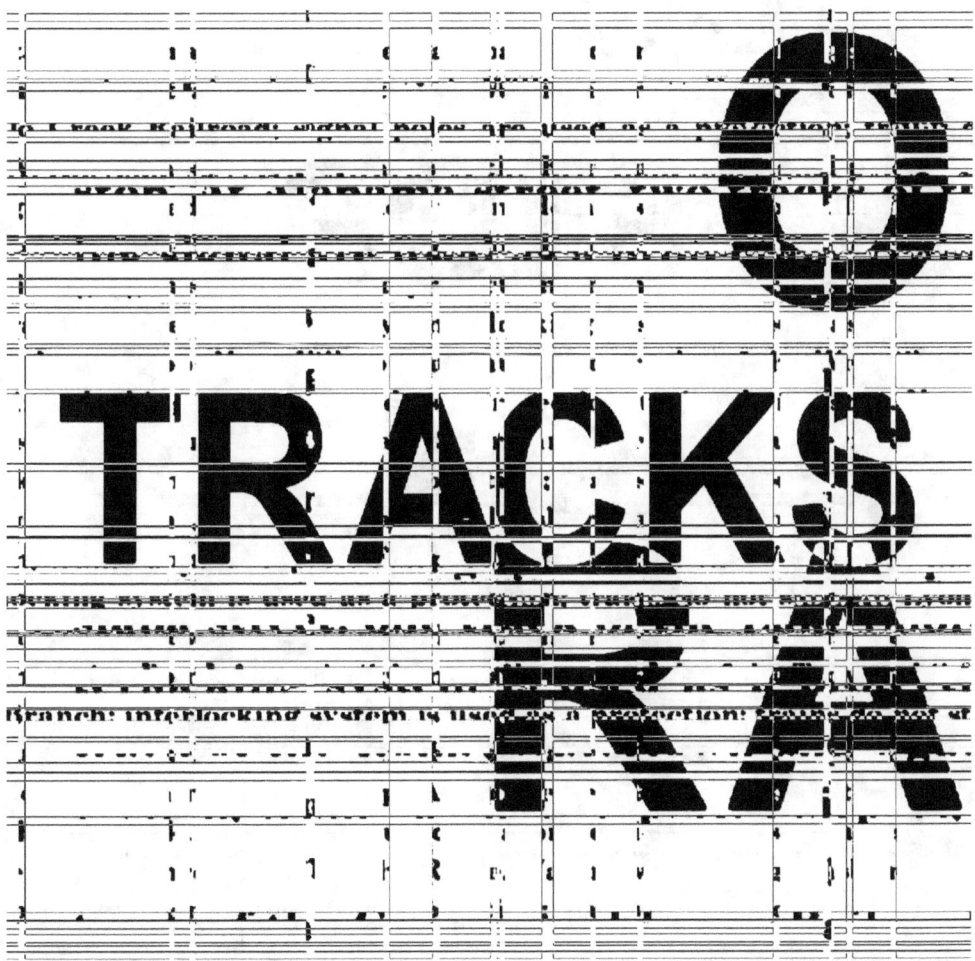

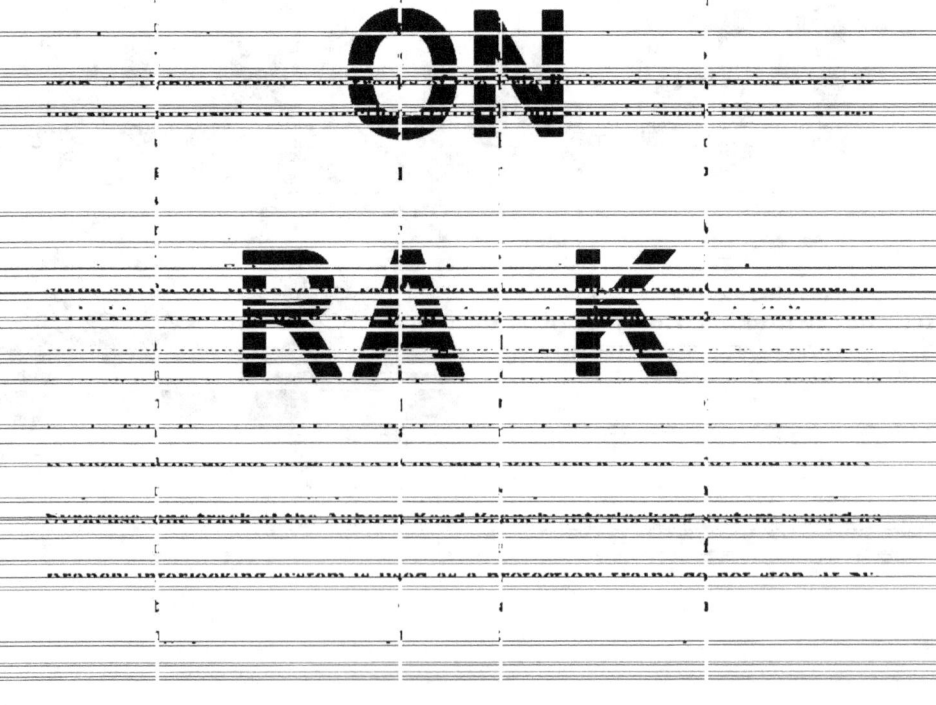

DO   O

S OP

N

T A KS

At Batavia one track of the Erie Railroad, and an interlocking system is used
as a protection; trains do not stop. At Brockport, one track of the
Buffalo Creek Railroad; signal water tank and a mechanical device is used
stop. At Allen Street, two tracks of the ... Second ... with the
the signal are used as a protection; trains do not stop. At South Division Street,
...
tection; trains do not stop. At Fairport, one track of the West Shore Railroad;
interlocking system is used as a protection; trains do not stop. At Lyons, one
track of the ... and Lyons Railroad; interlocking system is used as a pro-
...
branch; interlocking system is used as a protection; trains do not stop. At Sy-
...

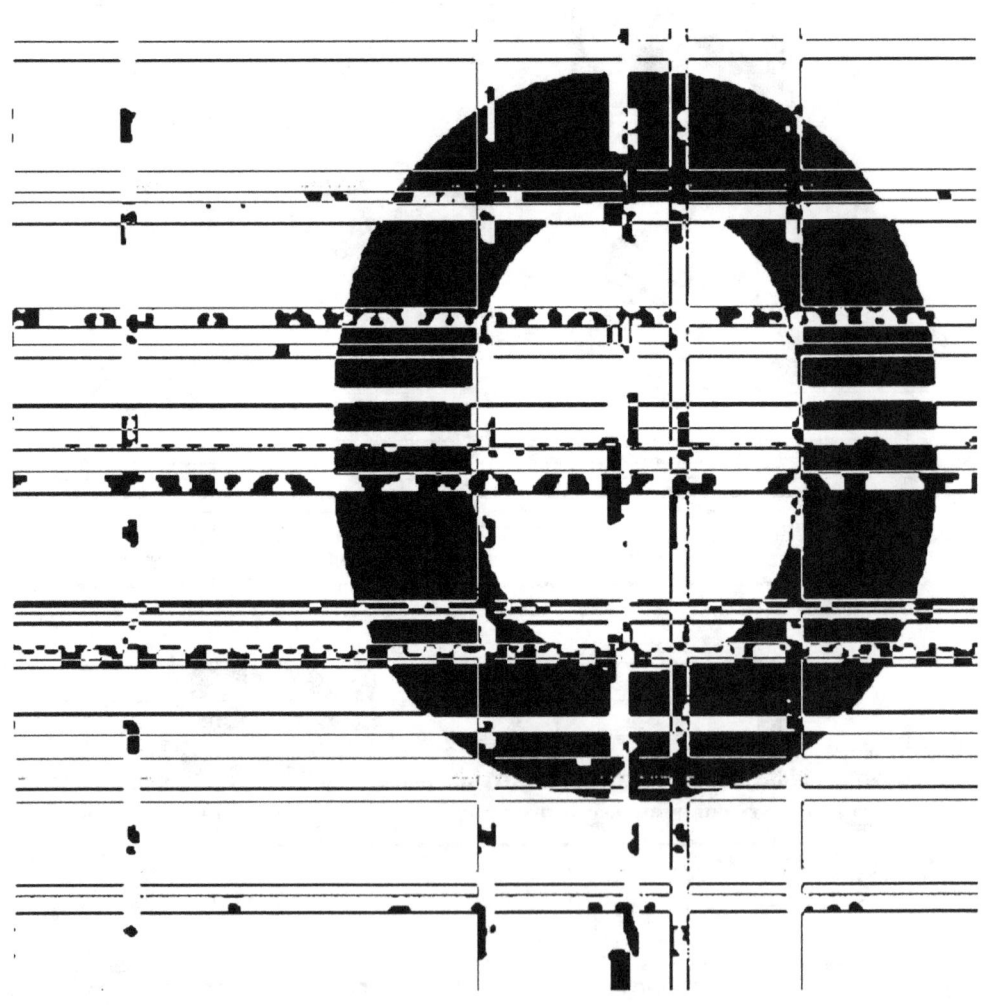

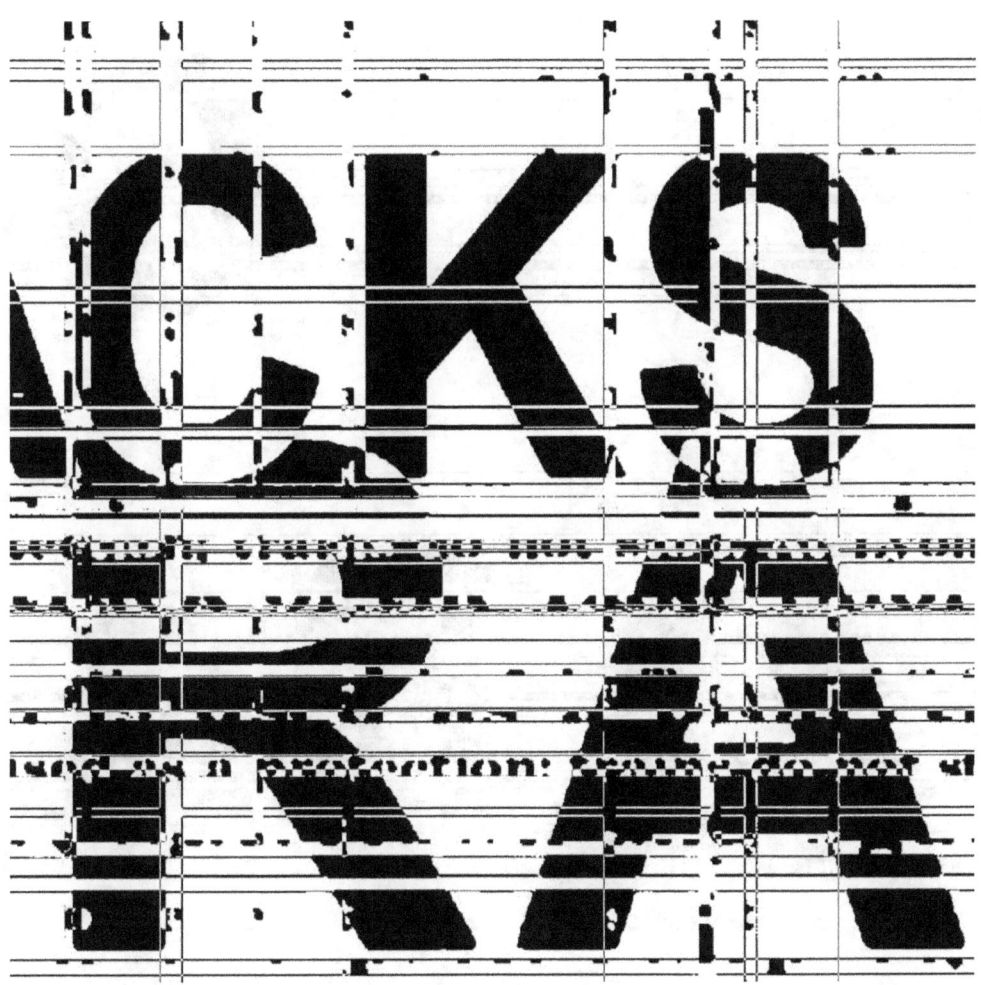

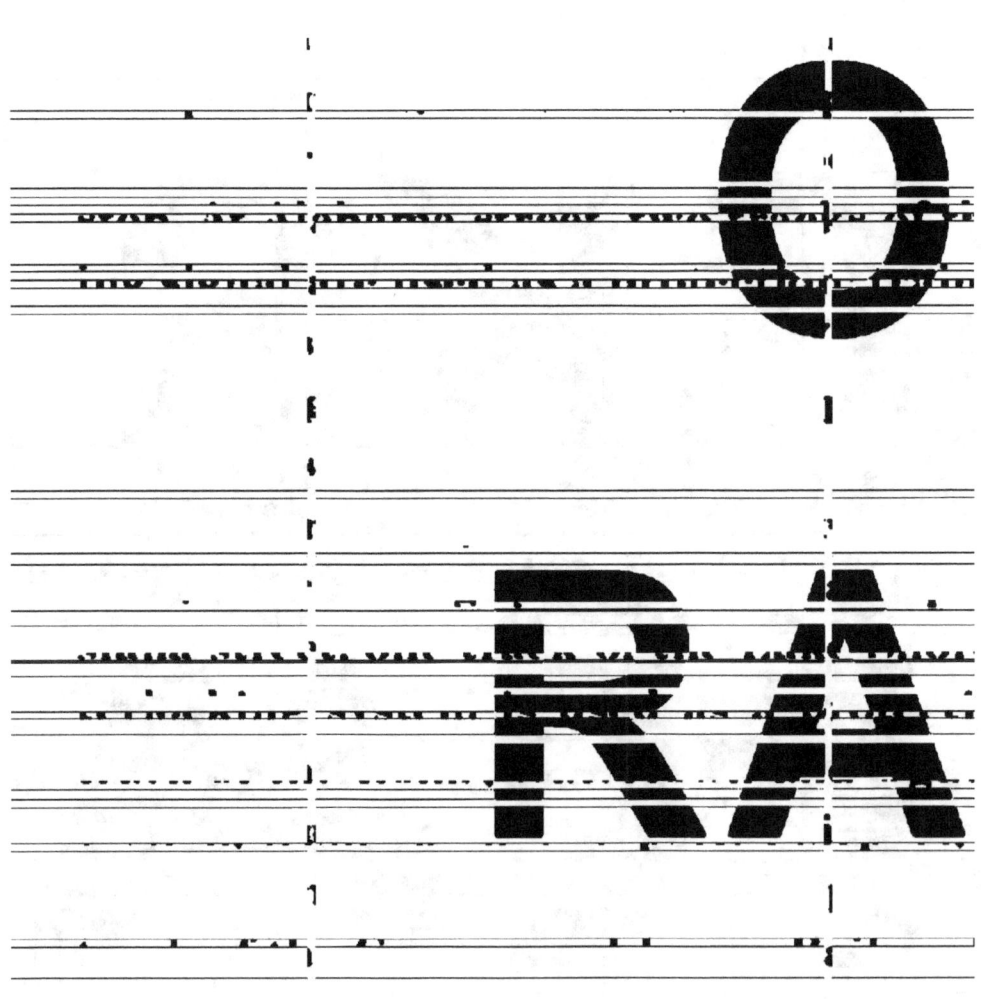

T A

tection: trains do not stop. At Fairport, one trac

interlocking system is used as a protection; trai

branch: interlocking system is used as a protect

KTSA

tection: trains do not stop. At Fairport, one trac

interlocking system is used as a protection; trai

branch: interlocking system is used as a protec

tection: trains do not stop. A

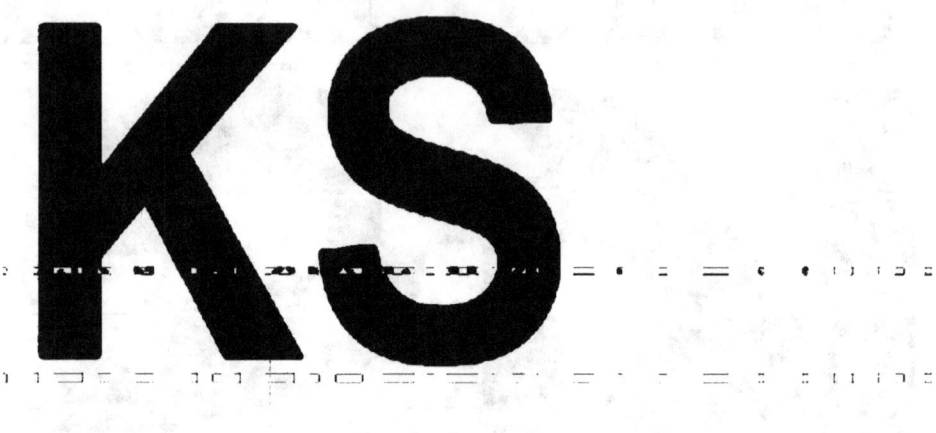

RAC

Rome, Watertown and Ogdensburg

RASC

Ro ne Wateros n and Ogdensburg ...

rdensburg; ...

... n ed tr c s t the Rome, Waterto n a d

ne, Waterto n a d gden bu ...

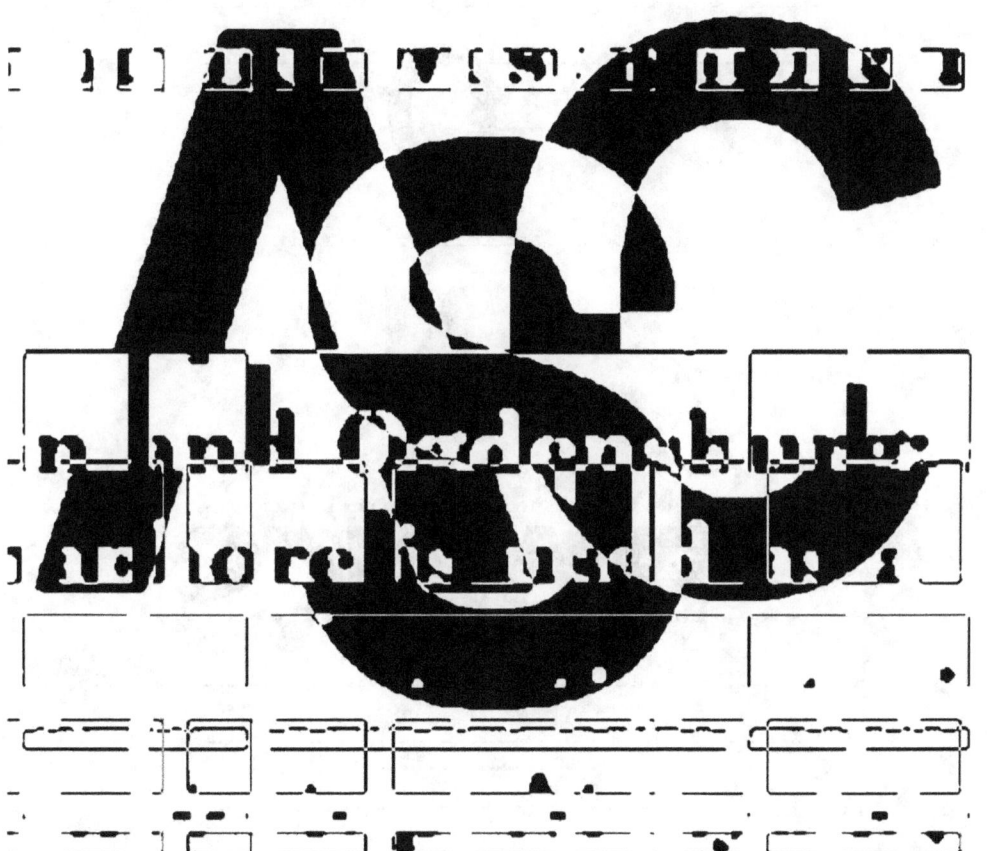

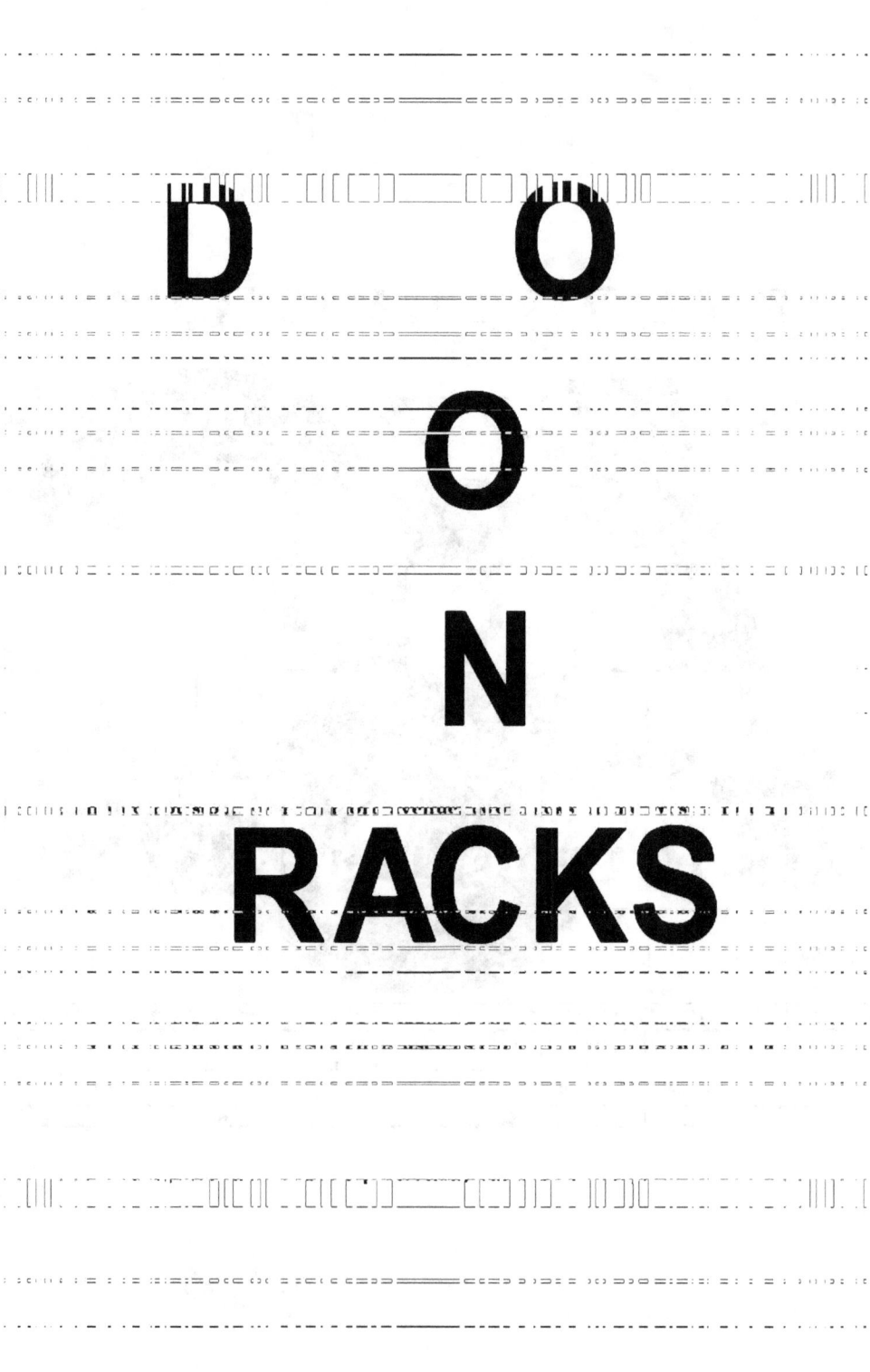

the Rome, Watertown and Ogdensburg ... semaphore is used ...

the Rome, Watertown and Ogdensburg ...

S

zdensburg: semaphore is used

ne, Watertown and ogdensburg

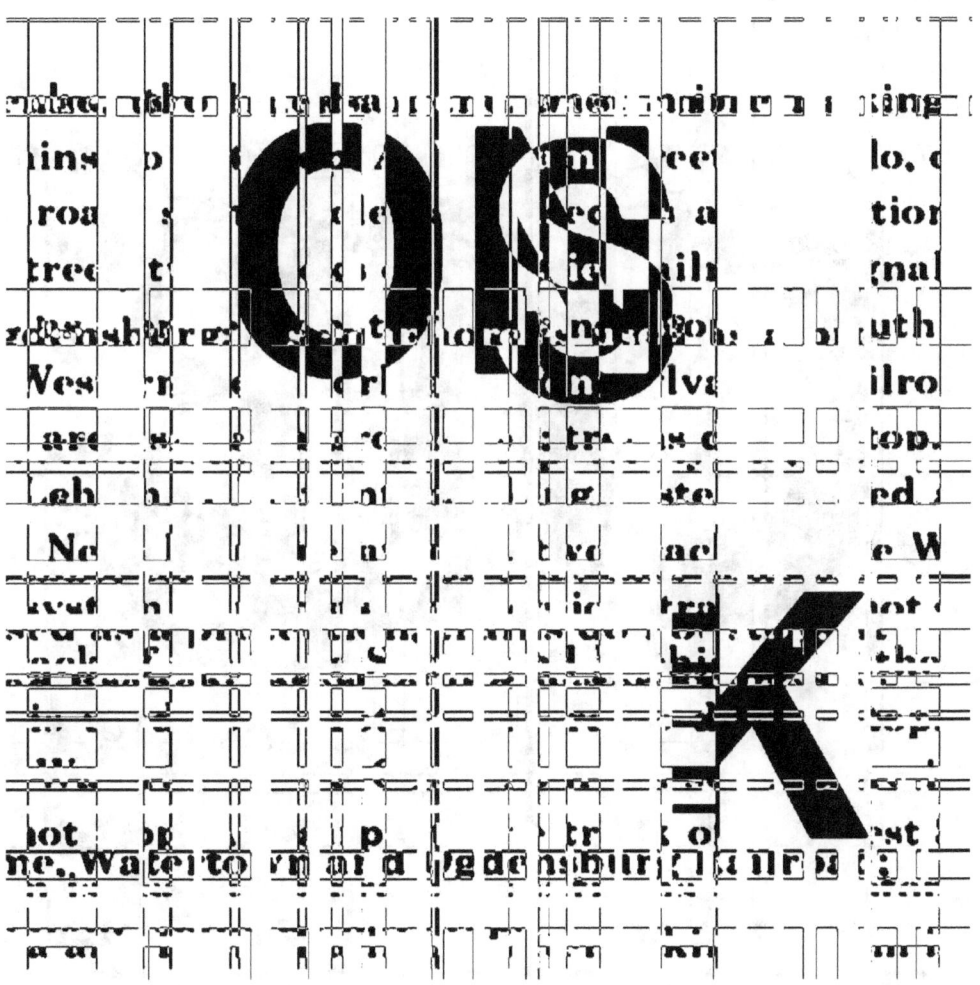

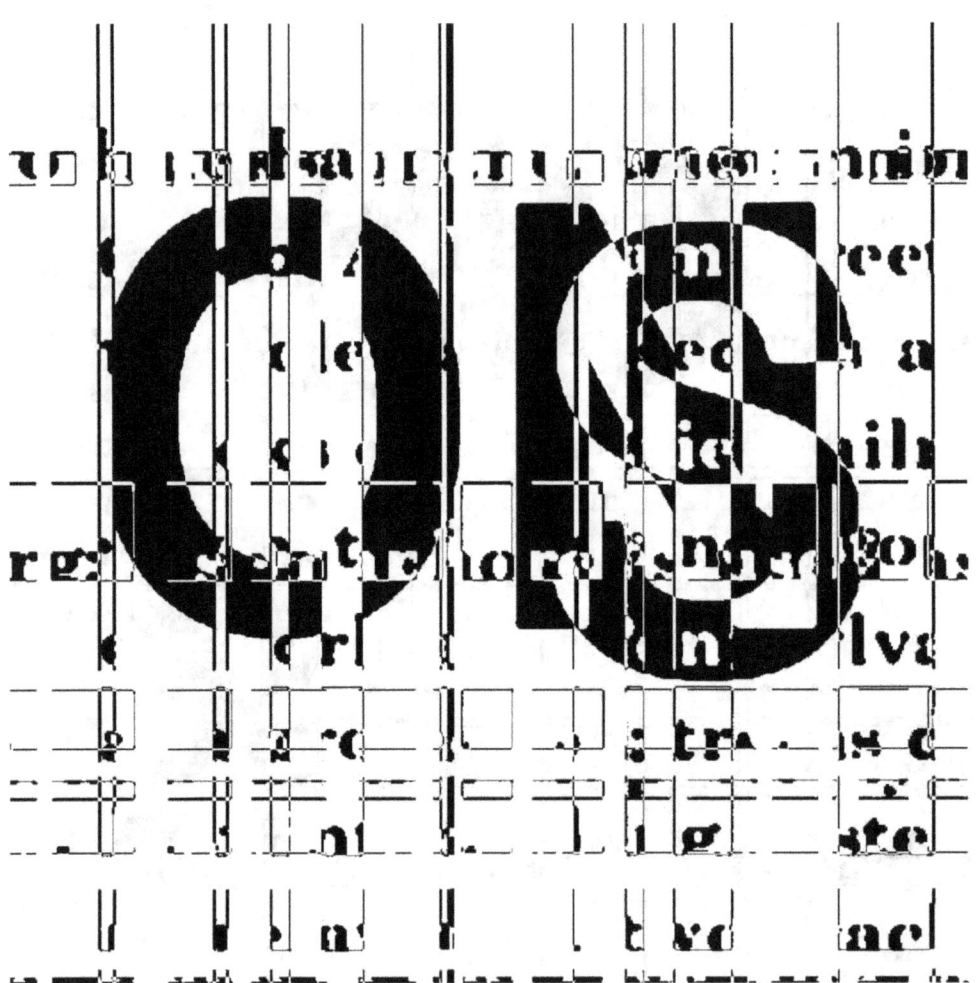

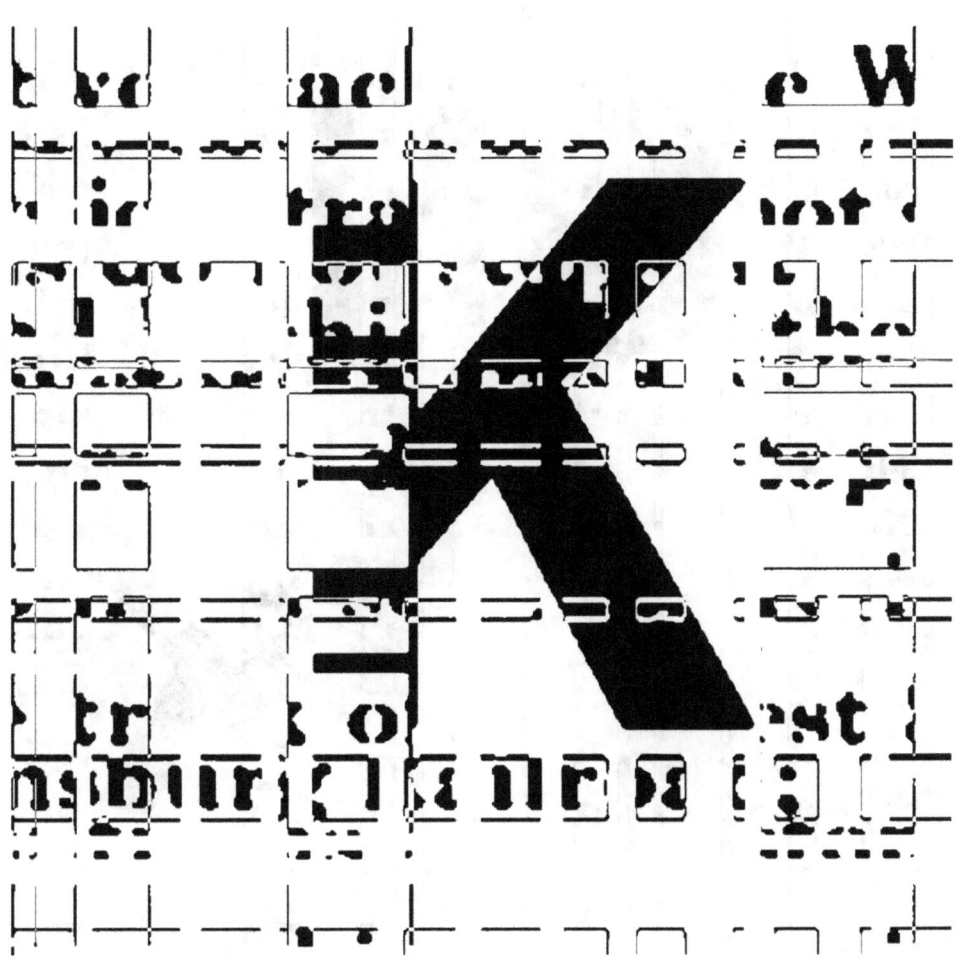

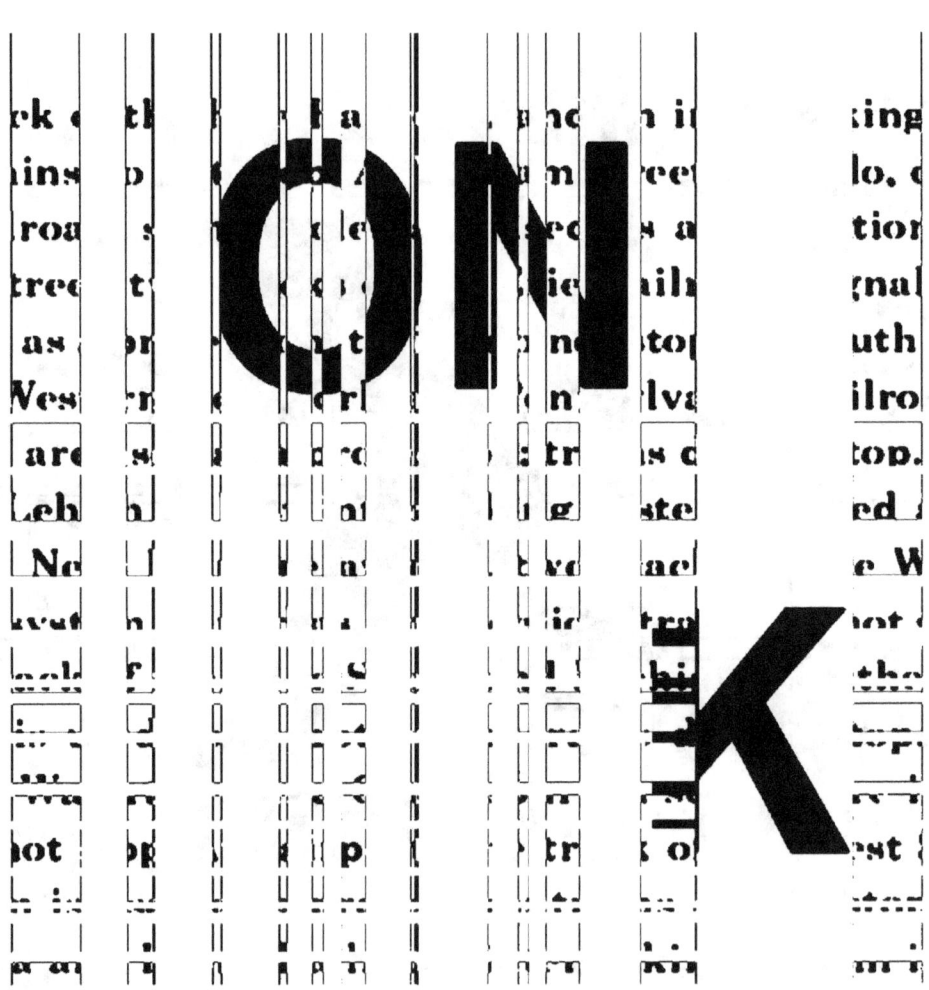

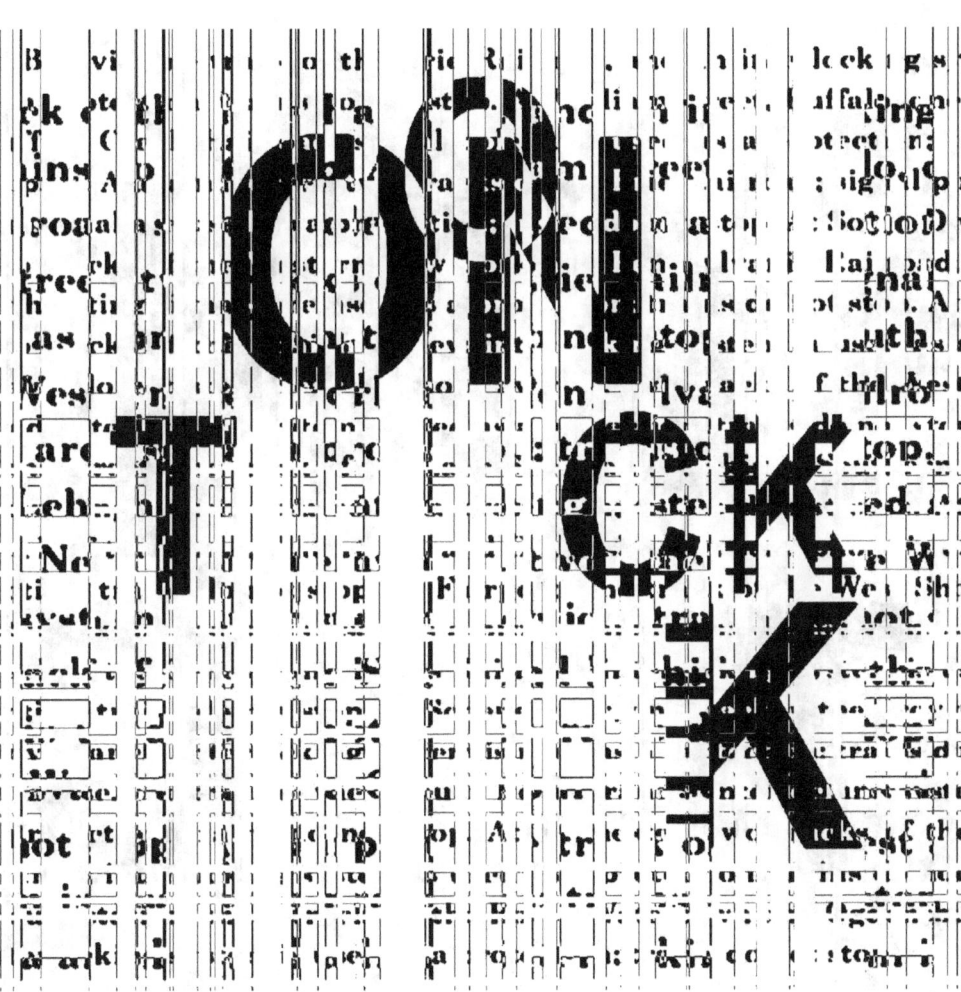

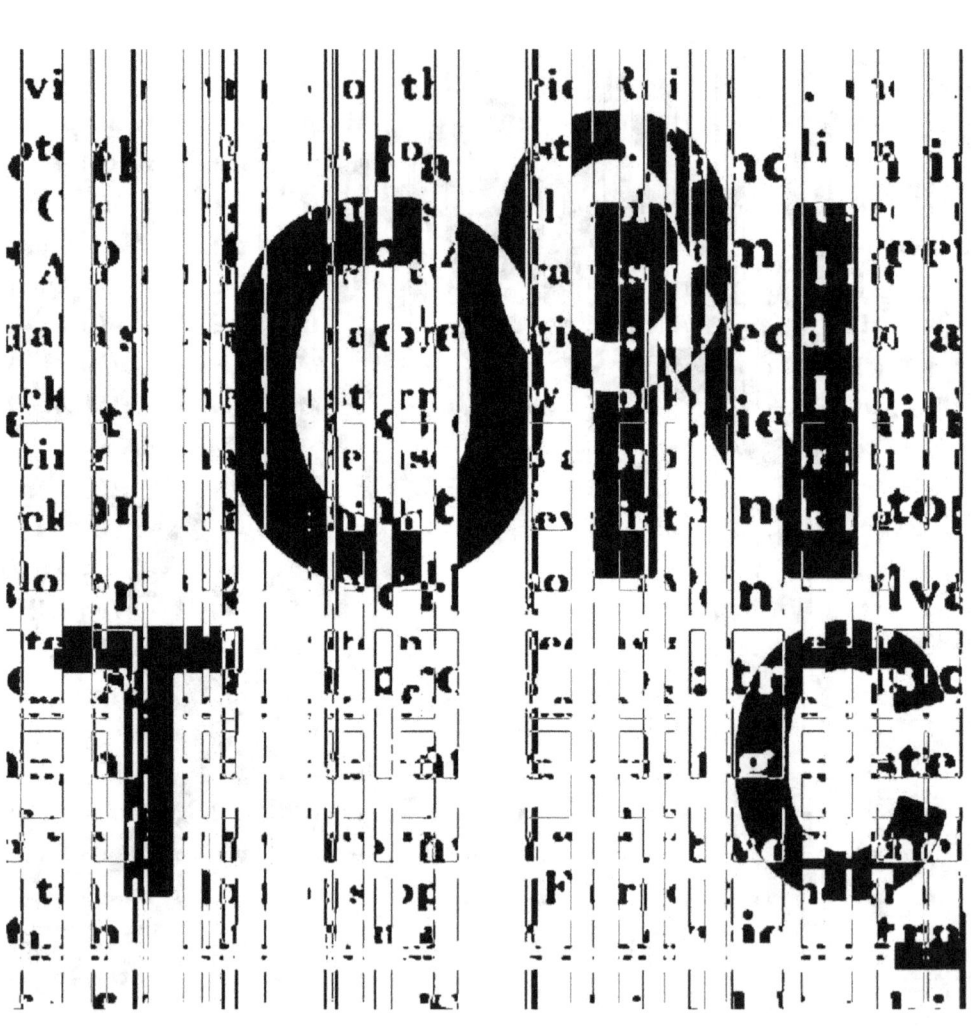

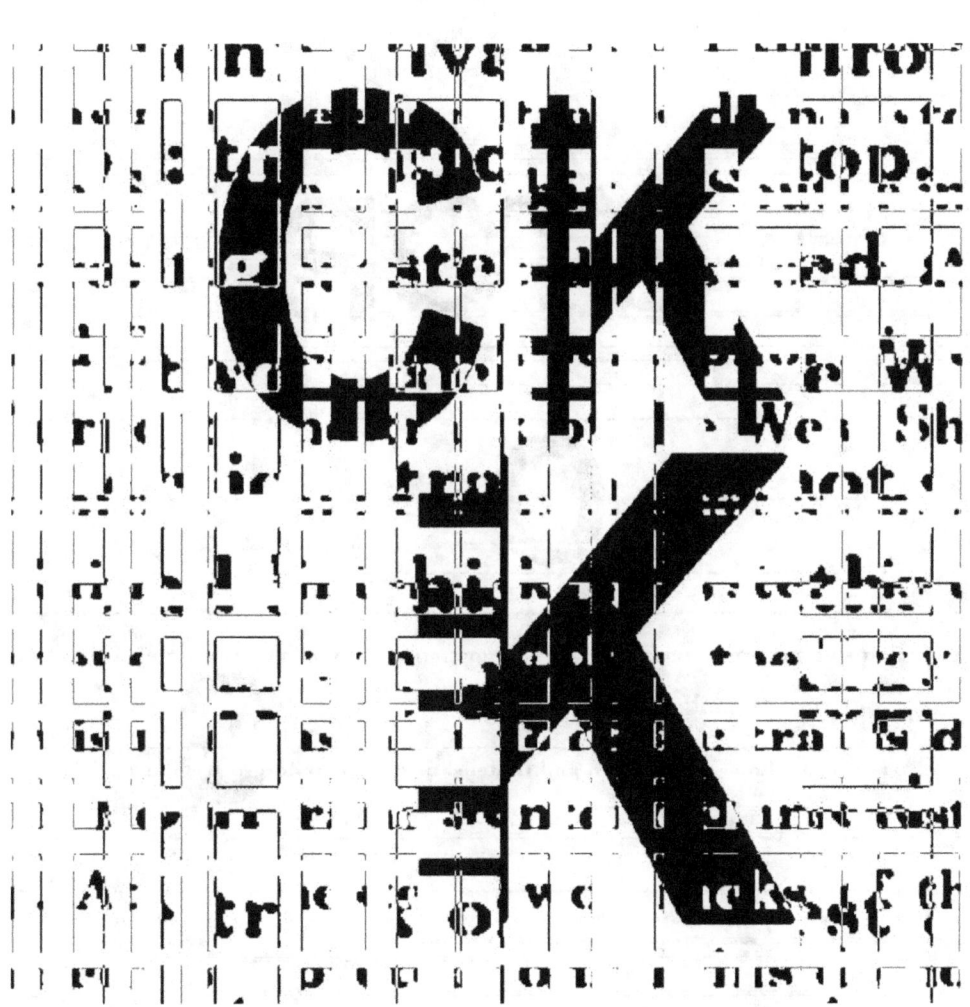

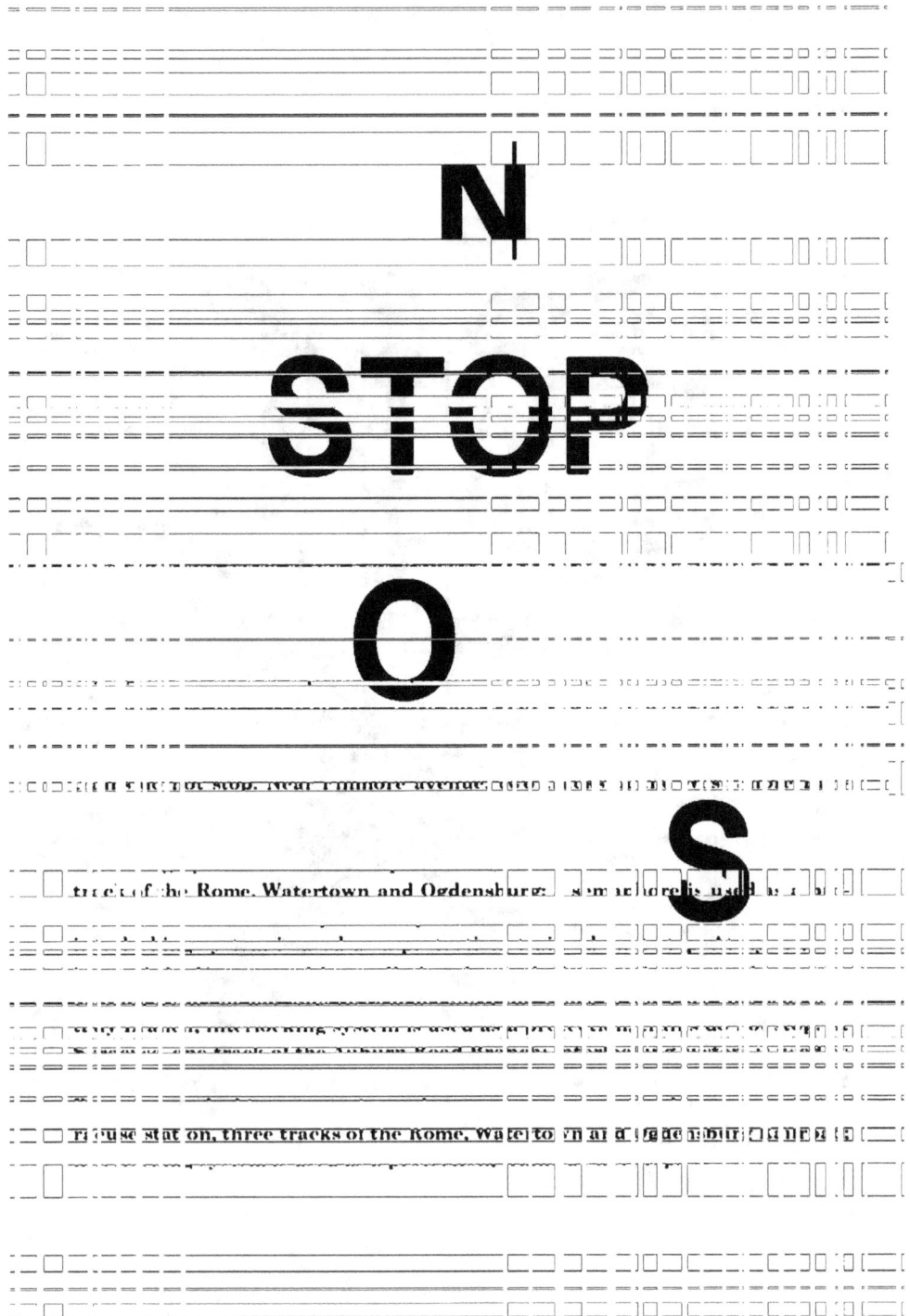

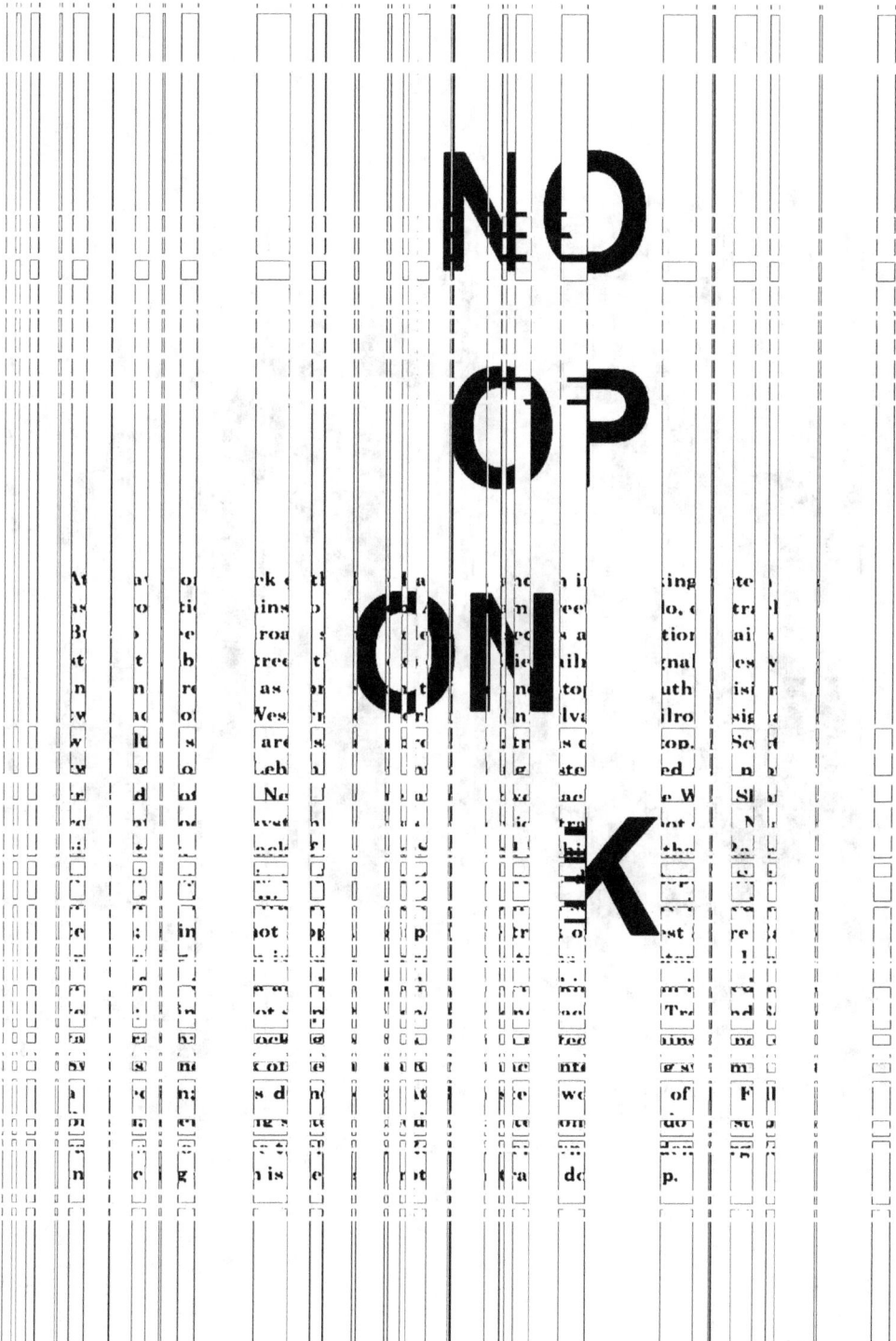

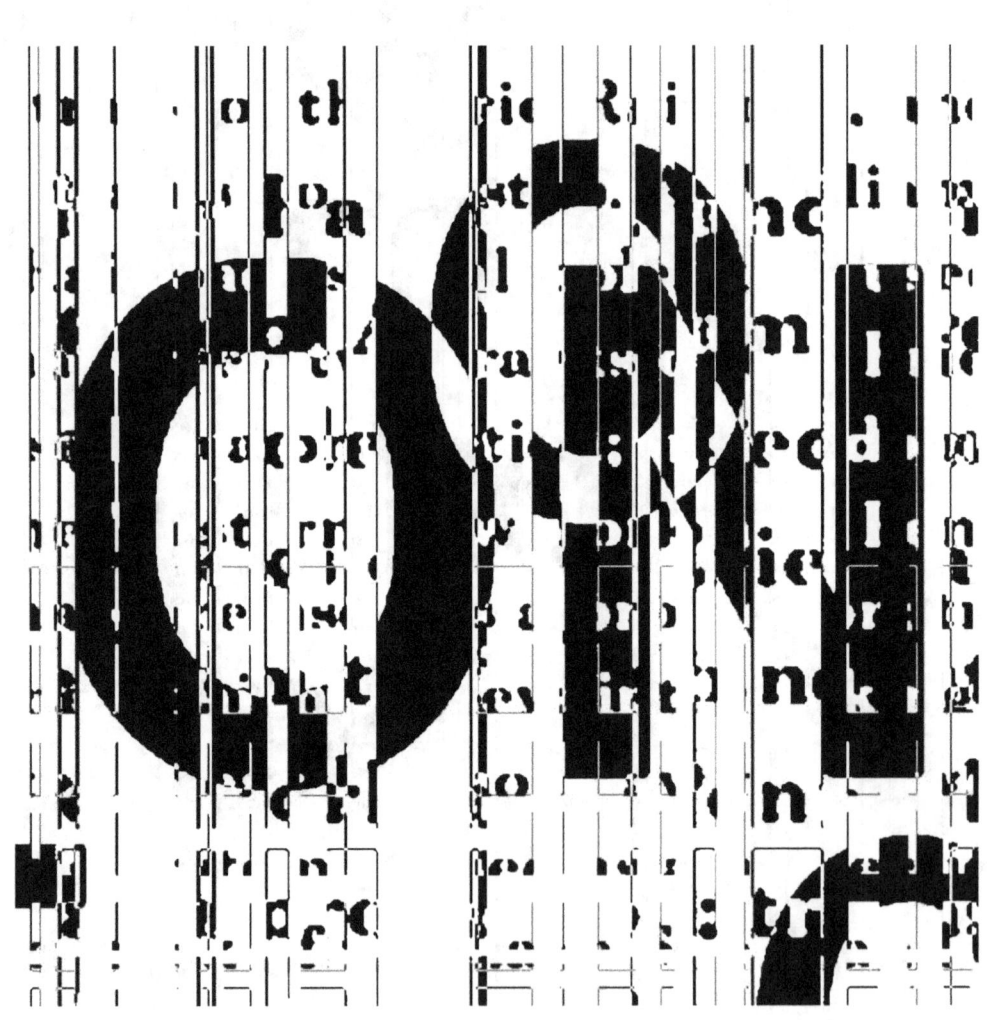

O

T I CK

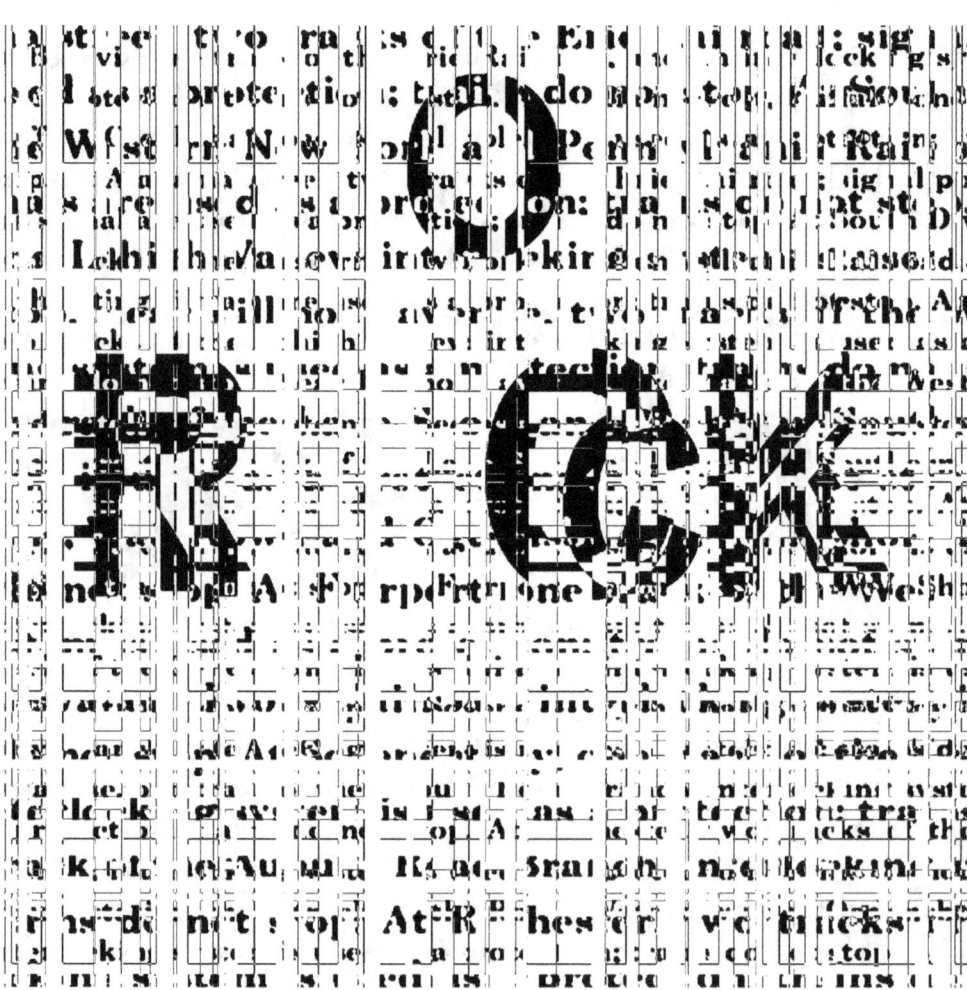

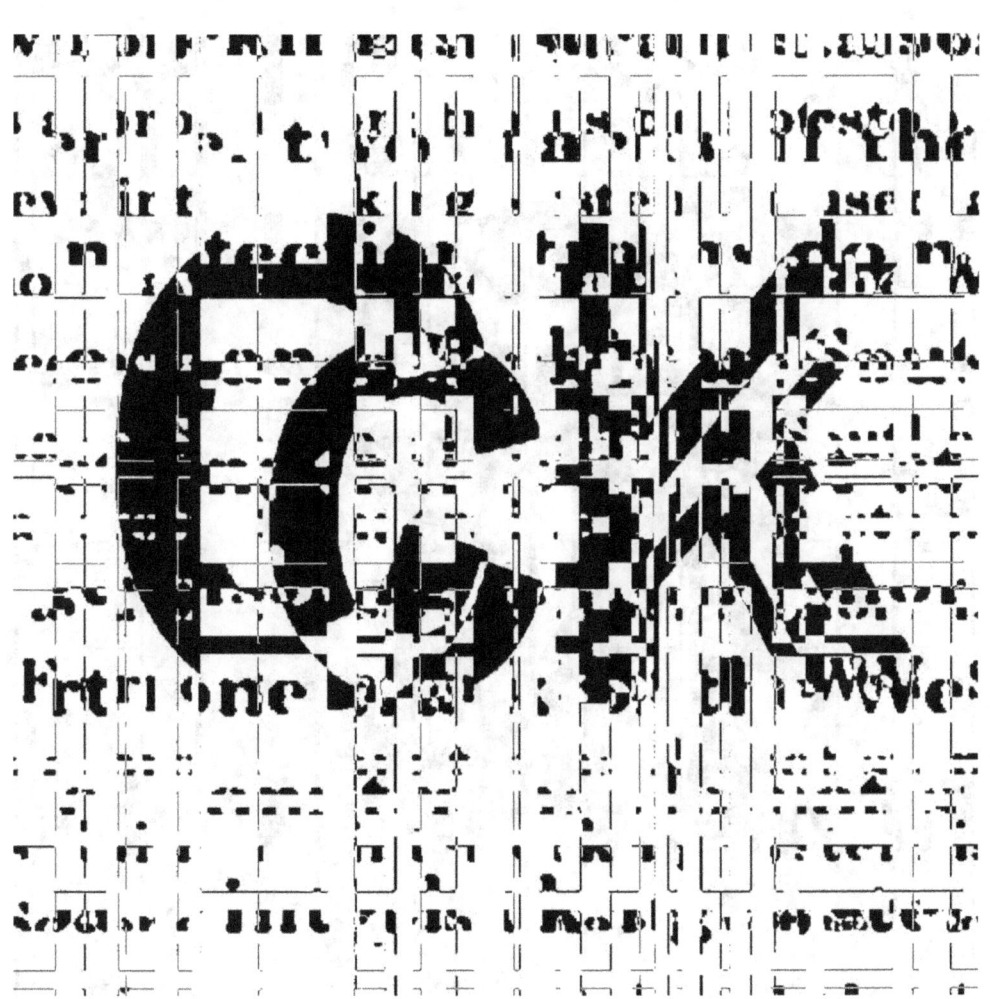

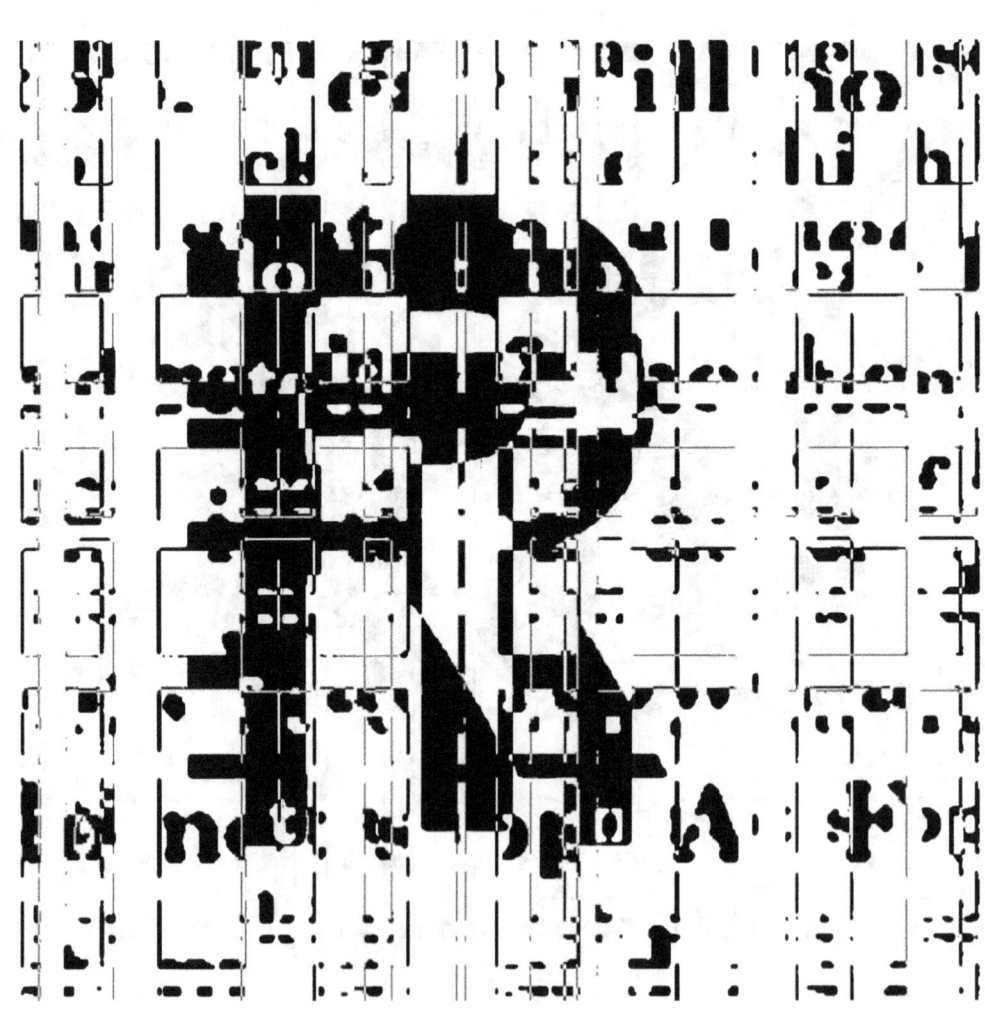

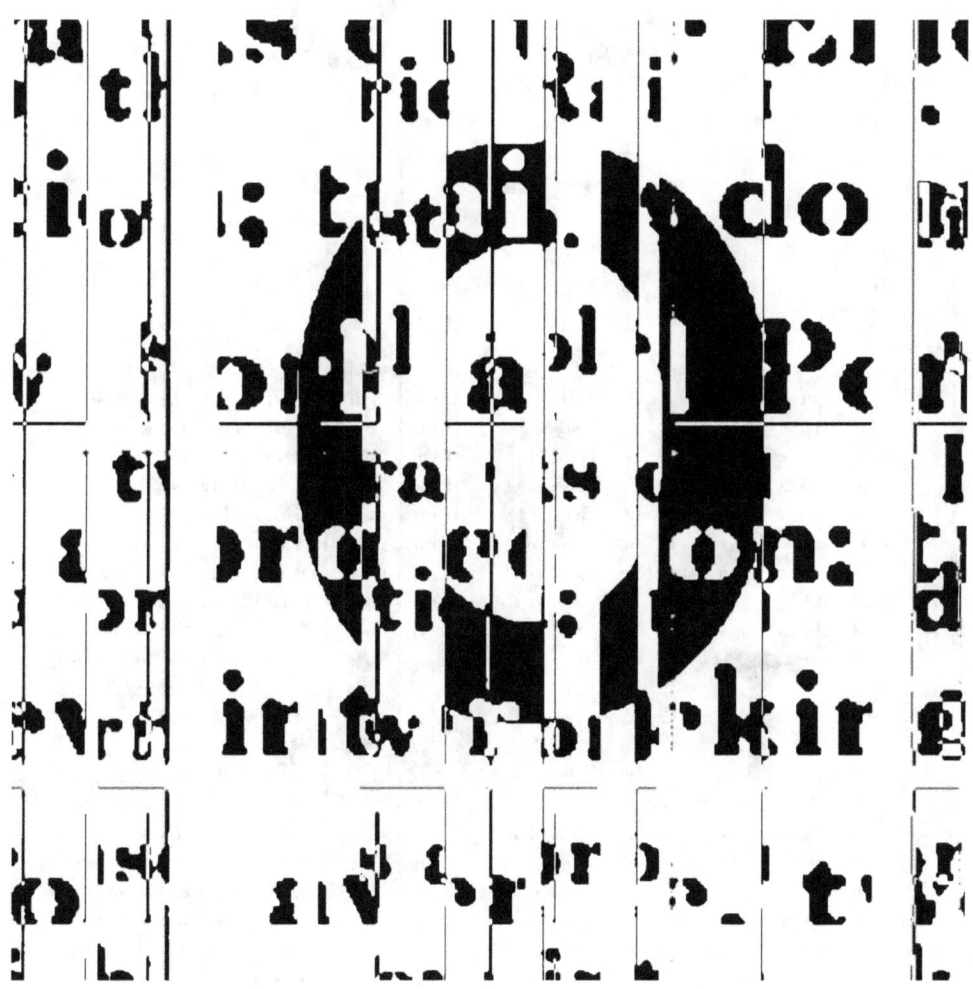

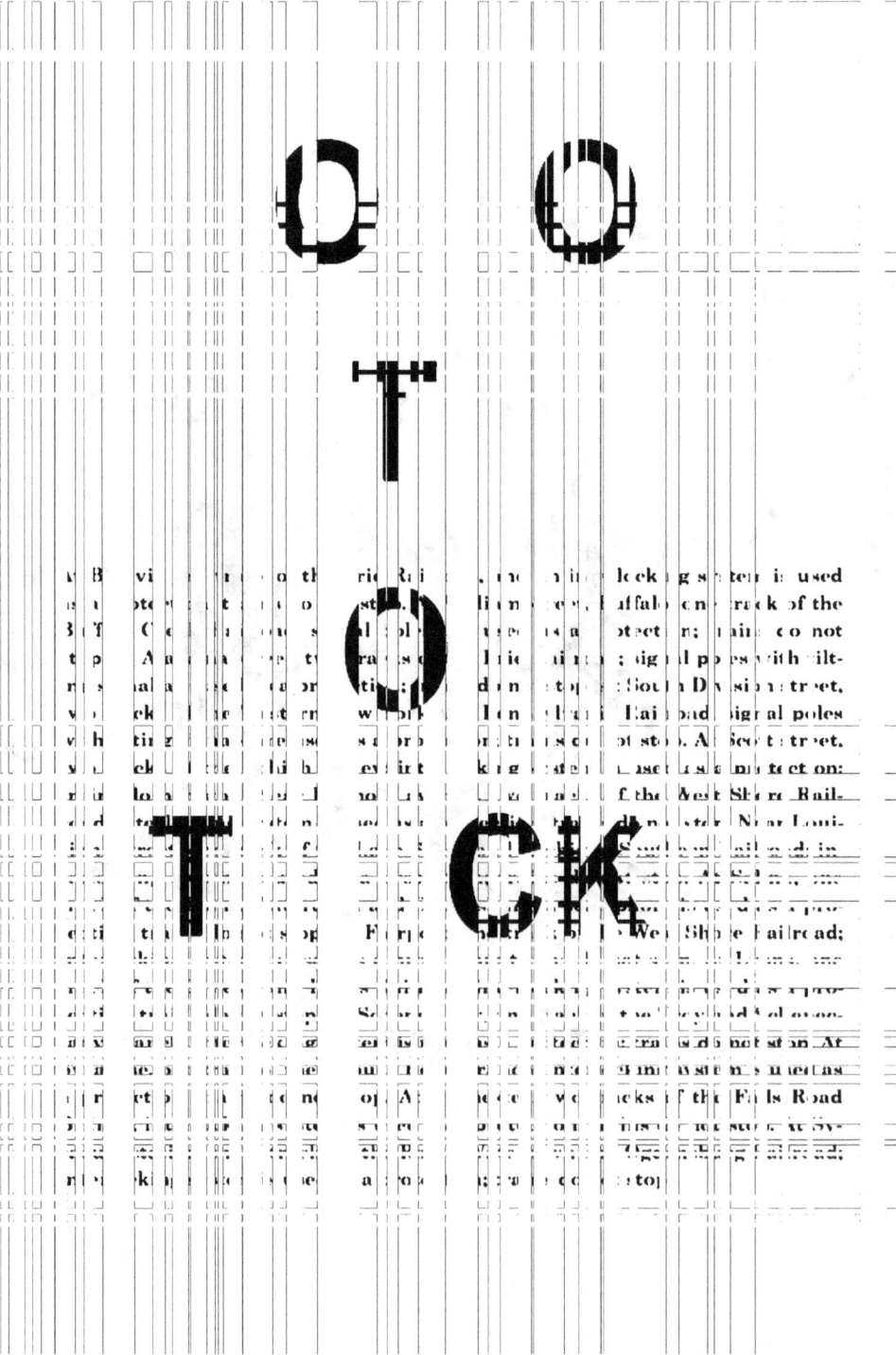

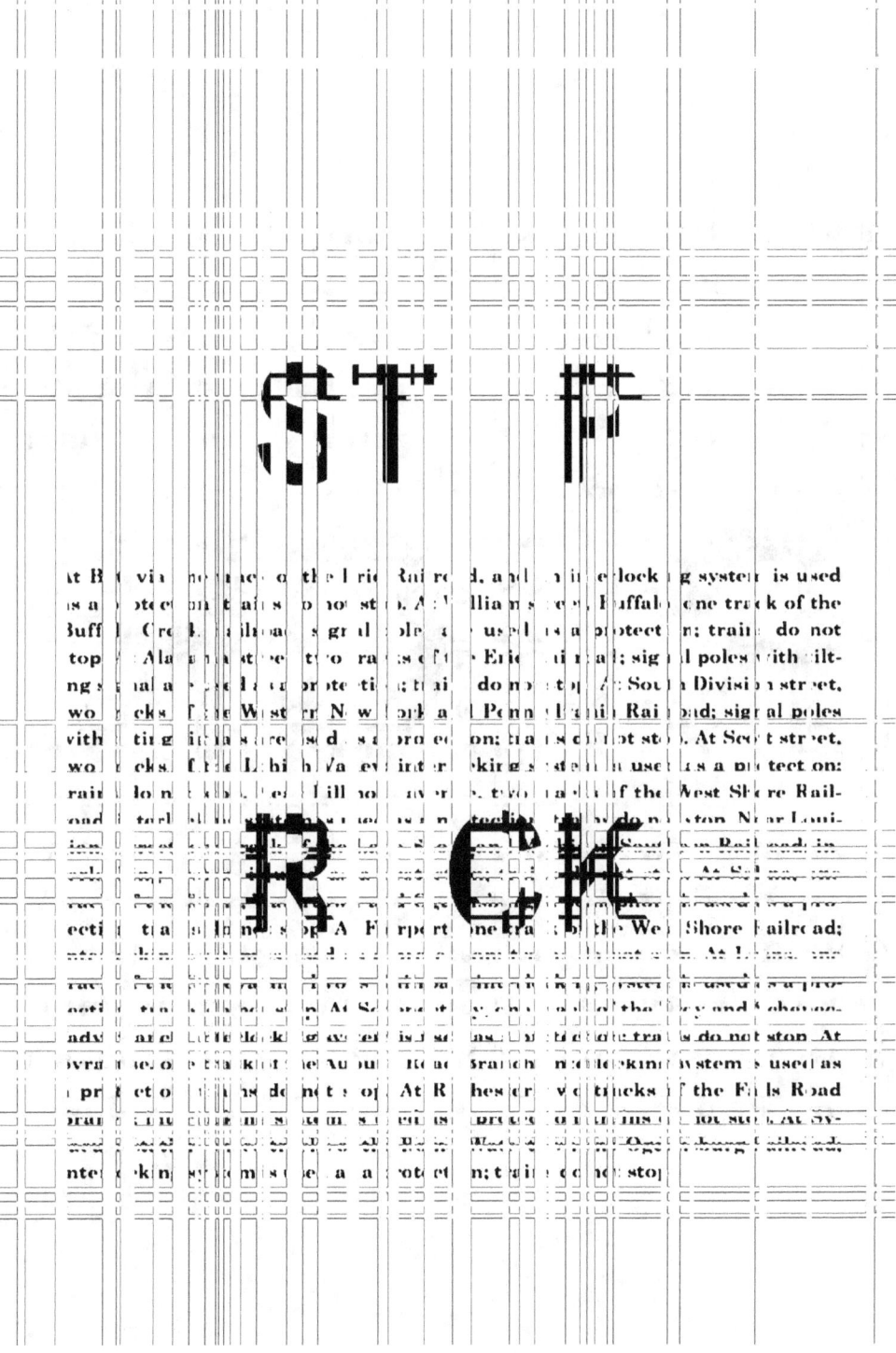

STP

RCK

At B via no ne o the Erie Railroad, and an interlocking system is used as a protection trains do not stop. At Williams street, Buffalo, one track of the Buffalo Creek Railroad is signal poles are used as a protection; trains do not stop. At Alabama street two tracks of the Erie railroad; signal poles with tilting signals are used as a protection; trains do not stop. At South Division street, two tracks of the Western New York and Pennsylvania Railroad; signal poles with tilting lights are used as a protection; trains do not stop. At Scott street, two tracks of the Lehigh Valley; an interlocking system is used as a protection; trains along track will not overe, two tracks of the West Shore Railroad interlocking is used protecting trains do not stop. Near Louis...

ecti trains will not stop. At Freeport one track of the West Shore Railroad;

At R hes dr ve tracks of the Falls Road
interlocking systems used as a protection; trains do not stop

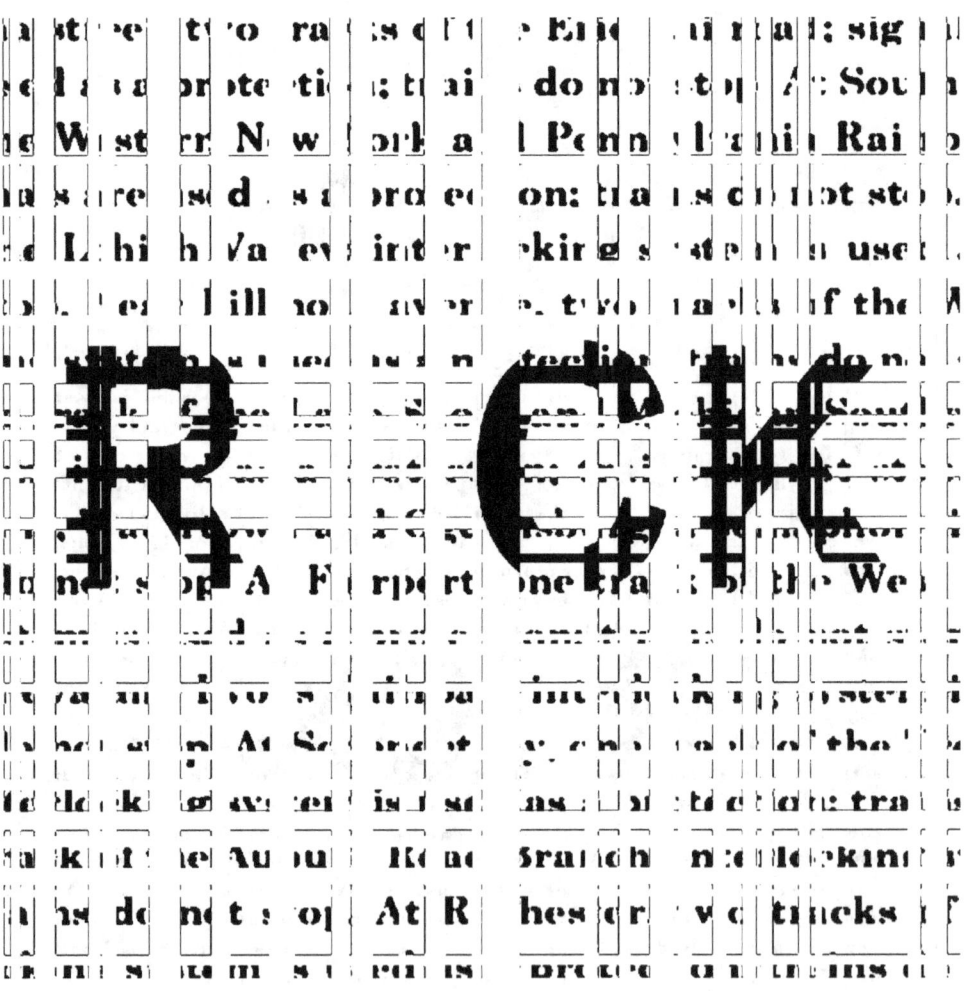

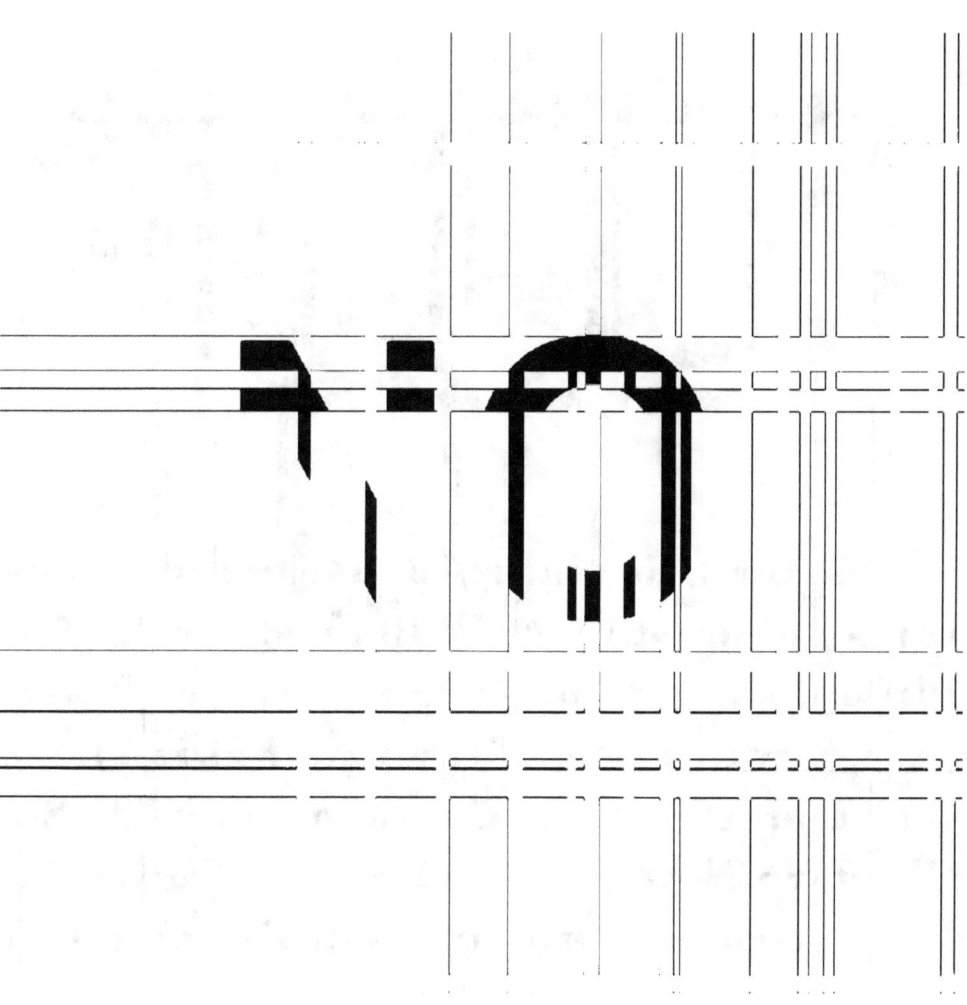

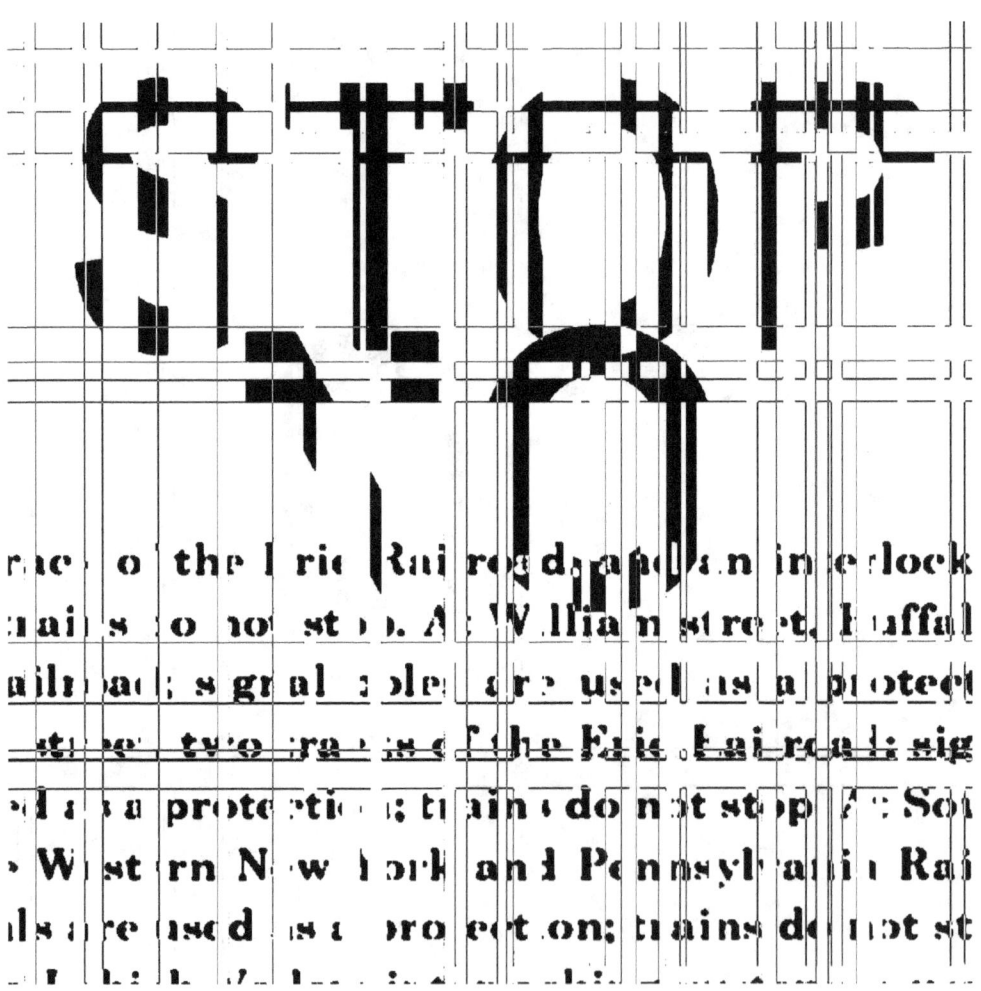

...rac...o...the...Erie Railroad, and an interlock...
......ails...do...not stop. At William street, Buffal...
...ailroad; signal poles...are used as a protect...
...een...two...racks of the Erie Railroad; sig...
...d as a protection; trains do not stop. At Sou...
...Western New York and Pennsylvania Rai...
...ls are used as a protection; trains do not st...
...

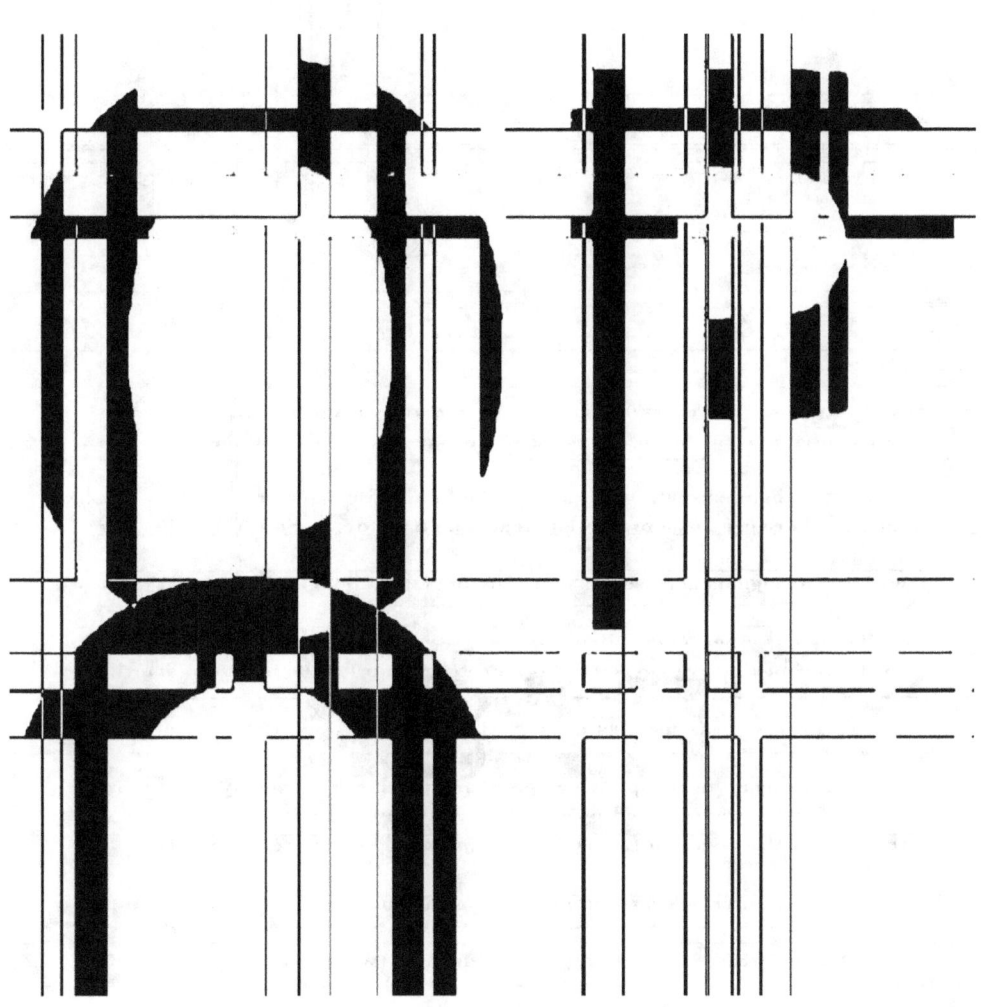

At railway one track of the Erie Railroad, and a interlocking system is used
as a protection; trains do not stop. At William street ...

stop. At Alabama street, two tracks of the Erie Railroad; signal poles with the
ing signal are used as a protection; trains do not stop. At South Division street

with tilting signals are used as a protection; trains do not stop. At ... street

road; interlocking system is used as a protection; trains do not stop. Near Lou

terlocking system is used as a protection; trains do not stop. At ...

tection; trains do not stop. At Fairport, one track of the West Shore Railroad

trict of the Geneva and Lyons Railroad; interlocking system is used ... pro

tady Branch; interlocking system is used as a protection; trains do not stop. A

a protection; trains do not stop. At Rochester, two tracks of the ... Rail

TION

RACK

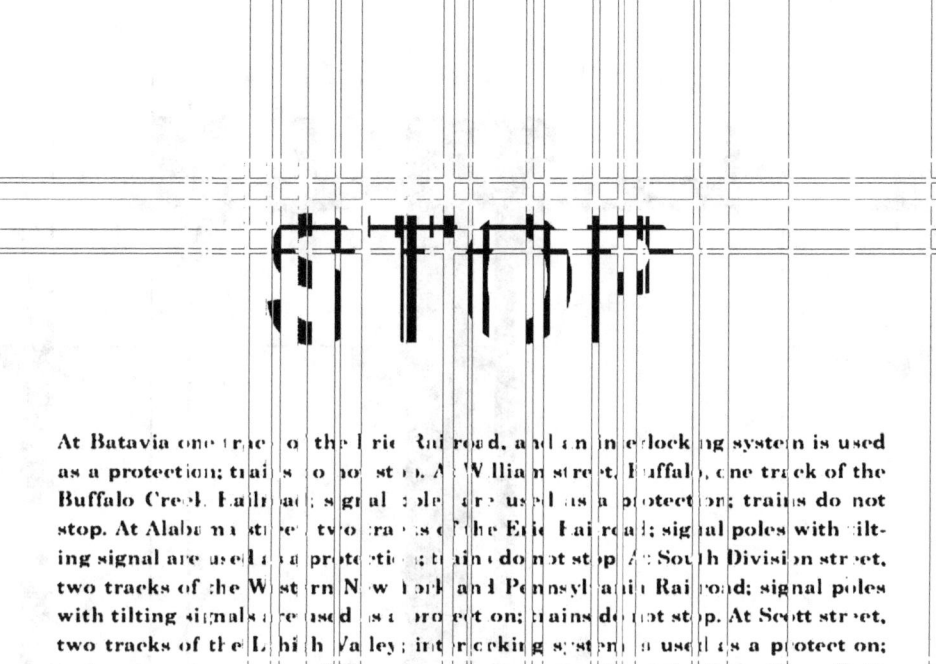

At Batavia one track of the Erie Railroad, and an interlocking system is used as a protection; trains do not stop. At William street, Buffalo, one track of the Buffalo Creek Railroad; signal poles are used as a protection; trains do not stop. At Alabama street, two tracks of the Erie Railroad; signal poles with tilting signal are used as a protection; trains do not stop. At South Division street, two tracks of the Western New York and Pennsylvania Railroad; signal poles with tilting signals are used as a protection; trains do not stop. At Scott street, two tracks of the Lehigh Valley; interlocking system is used as a protection; trains do not stop. Near Hill no avenue, two tracks of the West Shore Railroad; interlocking system is used as a protection; trains do not stop. Near Louisiana street, one track of the Lake Shore and Michigan Southern Railroad; interlocking system is used as a protection; trains do not stop. At Buffalo, one track of the Buffalo, New York and Philadelphia; interlocking is used as a protection; trains do not stop. At Fairport, one track of the West Shore Railroad; interlocking system is used as a protection; trains do not stop. At Lyons, one track of the Geneva and Lyons Railroad; interlocking system is used as a protection; trains do not stop. At Scotia station, one track of the Troy and Schenectady Branch; interlocking system is used as a protection; trains do not stop. At Syracuse, one track of the Auburn Road Branch; interlocking system is used as a protection; trains do not stop. At Rochester, two tracks of the Falls Road Branch; interlocking system is used as a protection; trains do not stop. At Syracuse station, third track of the Rome, Watertown and Ogdensburg Railroad; interlocking system is used as a protection; trains do not stop

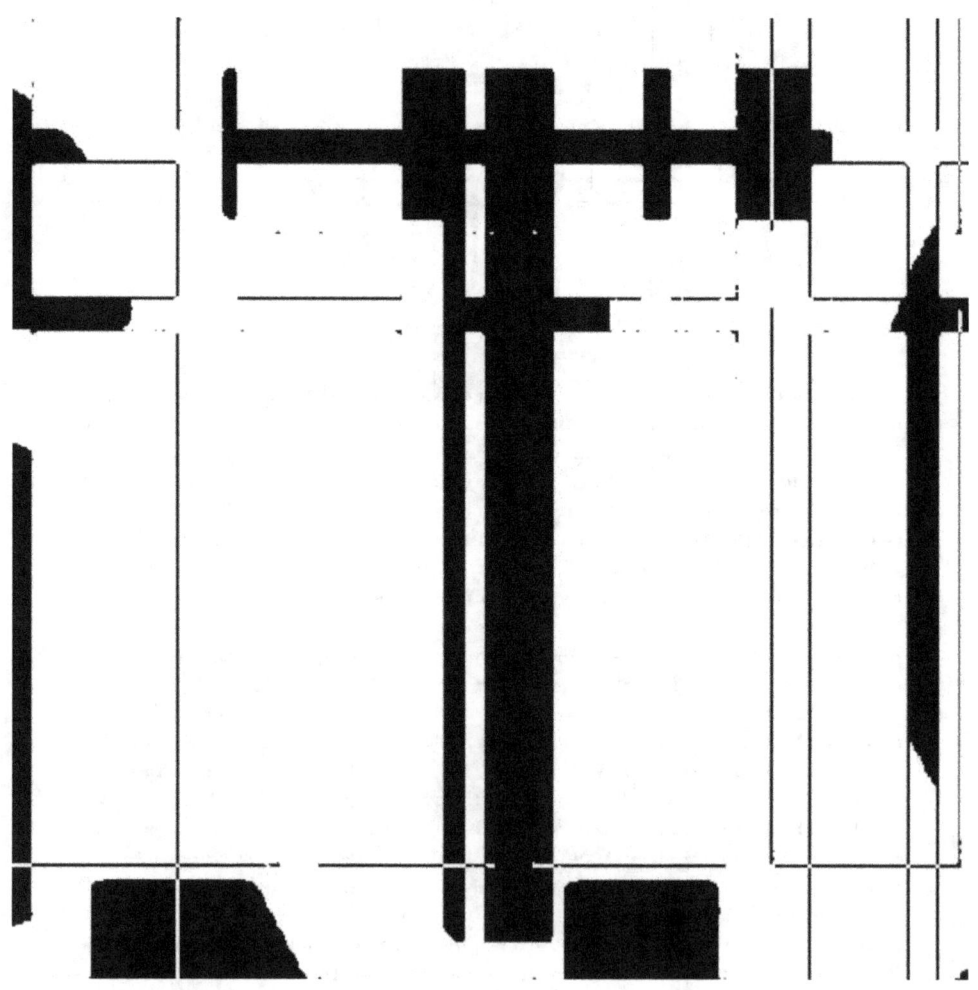

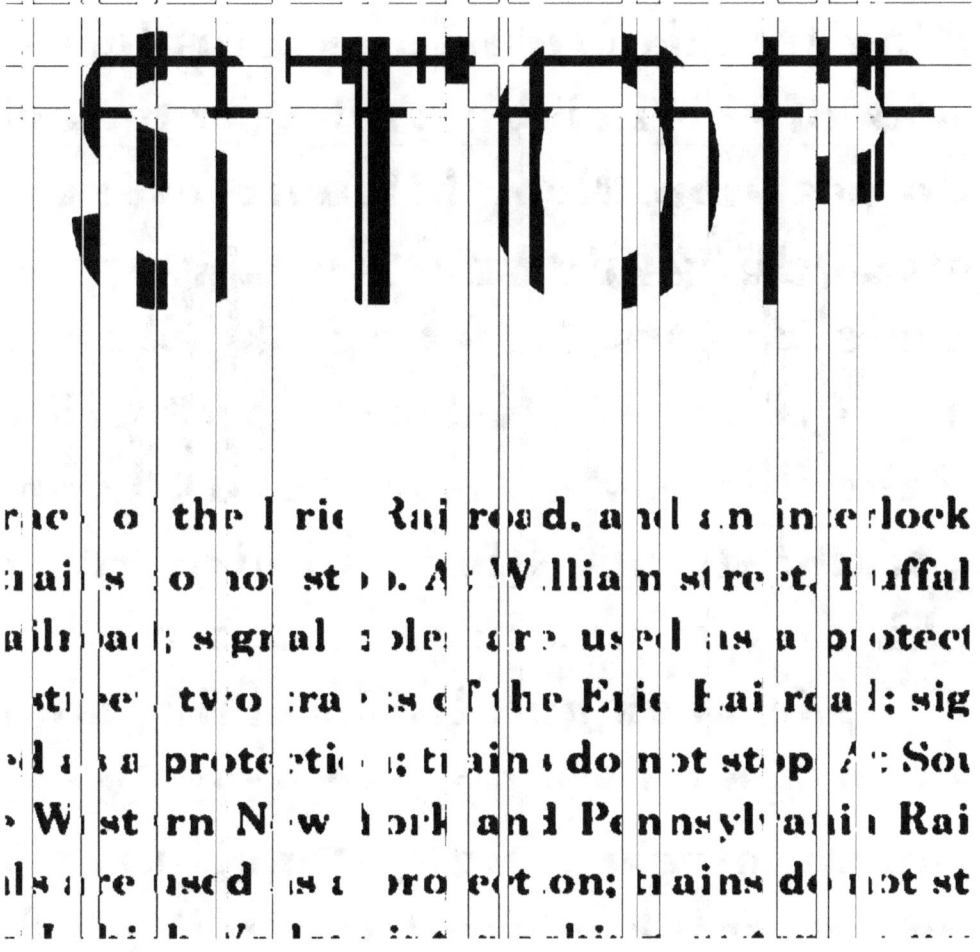

lting signals are used as a protectio

acks of the Lehigh Valley; inter.cel

do not stop. Near Fillmore avenue,

nterlocking system is used. At a prot

street, one track of the Lake Shore a

king system is used as a protection

of the Rome, Watertown and Ogdens

; trains do not stop. At Fairport, on

cking system is used as a protectio

of the Geneva and Lyons Railroad; i

e trains do not stop. At Schenectady

ranch; interlocking system is used a

on one track of the Auburn Road R

trains do not stop. At Scott stre
lting signals are used as a protectio
ng system is used as a protectio
acks of the Lehigh Valley inter ce
wo tracks of the West Shore Ra

of the Geneva and Lyons Railroad; i
erlocking system is used as a p
ine track of the Troy and Schen
ranch; interlocking system is used a
a protection; trains do not stop.

At Batavia one track of the Erie Railroad, and an interlocking system is used as a protection; trains do not stop. At William street, Buffalo, one track of the Buffalo Creek Railroad signal poles are used as a protection; trains do not stop. At Alabama street, two tracks of the Erie Railroad; signal poles with tilting signal are used as a protection; trains do not stop. At South Division street, two tracks of the Western New York and Pennsylvania Railroad; signal poles with tilting signals are used as a protection; trains do not stop. At Scott street, two tracks of the Lehigh Valley; interlocking system is used as a protection; trains do not stop. Near Fillmore avenue, two tracks of the West Shore Railroad; interlocking system is used as a protection; trains do not stop. Near Louisiana street, one track of the Lake Shore and Michigan Southern Railroad; interlocking system is used as a protection; trains do not stop. At Salina, one track of the Rome, Watertown and Ogdensburg; a semaphore is used as a protection; trains do not stop. At Fairport, one track of the West Shore Railroad; interlocking system is used as a protection; trains do not stop. At Lyons, one track of the Geneva and Lyons Railroad; interlocking system is used as a protection; trains do not stop. At Schenectady, one track of the Troy and Schenectady Branch; interlocking system is used as a protection; trains do not stop. At Syracuse, one track of the Auburn Road Branch; interlocking system is used as a protection; trains do not stop. At Rochester, two tracks of the Falls Road Branch; interlocking system is used as a protection; trains do not stop. At Syracuse station, three tracks of the Rome, Watertown and Ogdensburg Railroad; interlocking system is used as a protection; trains do not stop

At Batavia one track of the Erie Railroad and an interlocking system is used as a protection; trains do not stop. At William street, Buffalo, one track of the Buffalo Creek Railroad; signal poles are used as a protection; trains do not stop. At Alabama street, two tracks of the Erie Railroad; signal poles with tilting signal are used as a protection; trains do not stop. At South Division street, two tracks of the Western New York and Pennsylvania Railroad signal poles with tilting signals are used as a protection; trains do not stop. At Scott street, two tracks of the Lehigh Valley; interlocking system is used as a protection; trains do not stop. Near Fillmore avenue, two tracks of the West Shore Railroad; interlocking system is used as a protection; trains do not stop. Near Louisiana street, one track of the Lake Shore and Michigan Southern Railroad; interlocking system is used as a protection; trains do not stop. At Salina, one track of the Rome, Watertown and Ogdensburg; a semaphore is used as a protection; trains do not stop. At Fairport, one track of the West Shore Railroad; interlocking system is used as a protection; trains do not stop. At Lyons, one track of the Geneva and Lyons Railroad; interlocking system is used as a protection; trains do not stop. At Schenectady, one track of the Troy and Schenectady Branch; interlocking system is used as a protection; trains do not stop. At Syracuse, one track of the Auburn Road Branch; interlocking system is used as a protection; trains do not stop. At Rochester, two tracks of the Falls Road Branch; interlocking system is used as a protection; trains do not stop. At Syracuse station, three tracks of the Rome, Watertown and Ogdensburg Railroad; interlocking system is used as a protection; trains do not stop.

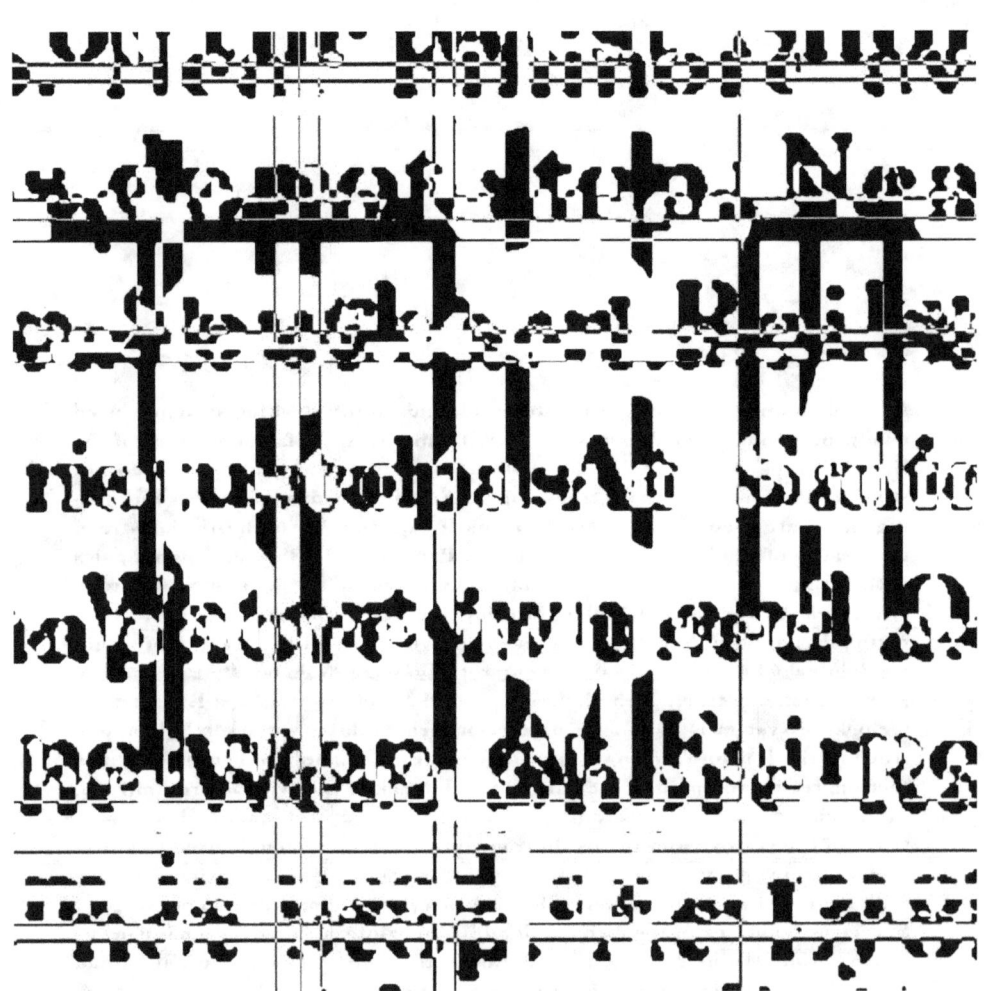

trains do no: stop. At Scott stre
ng system is used as a protectio
wo tracks of the West Shore Ra
tion; trains do not stop. Near Lo
d Michigan Southern Railroad;
trains do not stop. At Salina, o
urg; a semaphore is used as a pr
track of the West Shore Railroa
trains do not stop. At Lyons, o
terlocking system is used as a pr
 one track of the Troy and Schene
a protection; trains do not stop.

At Batavia one track of the Erie Railroad, and an interlocking system is used as a protection; trains do not stop. At William street, Buffalo, one track of the Buffalo Creek Railroad; signal poles are used as a protection; trains do not stop. At Alabama street, two tracks of the Erie Railroad; signal poles with tilting signal are used as a protection; trains do not stop. At South Division street, two tracks of the Western New York and Pennsylvania Railroad; signal poles with tilting signals are used as a protection; trains do not stop. At Scott street, two tracks of the Lehigh Valley; interlocking system is used as a protection; trains do not stop. Near Fillmore avenue, two tracks of the West Shore Railroad; interlocking system is used as a protection; trains do not stop. Near Louisiana street, one track of the Lake Shore and Michigan Southern Railroad; interlocking system is used as a protection; trains do not stop. At Salina, one track of the Rome, Watertown and Ogdensburg; a semaphore is used as a protection; trains do not stop. At Fairport, one track of the West Shore Railroad; interlocking system is used as a protection; trains do not stop. At Lyons, one track of the Geneva and Lyons Railroad; interlocking system is used as a protection; trains do not stop. At Schenectady, one track of the Troy and Schenectady Branch; interlocking system is used as a protection; trains do not stop. At Syracuse, one track of the Auburn Road Branch; interlocking system is used as a protection; trains do not stop. At Rochester, two tracks of the Falls Road Branch; interlocking system is used as a protection; trains do not stop. At Syracuse station, three tracks of the Rome, Watertown and Ogdensburg Railroad; interlocking system is used as a protection; trains do not stop.

Acknowledgments

This sequence is based on Regulatory Sign R8-8 from the *Manual on Uniform Traffic Control Devices* (MUTCD), published by the USDOT Federal Highway Administration. I have also used text from the *Sixteenth Annual Report of the Board of Railroad Commissioners of the State of New York, for the Year 1898.*

Excerpts have appeared in *Utsanga, Eratio Poetry Journal,* and *Out of Nowhere.*

Special thanks to Joakim Norling, Robin Tomens, Toni Hanner, John M. Bennett, and C. Mehrl Bennett for helping or supporting this project, in one way or another.

And very special thanks to my wife and best friend, Lori.

www.ingramcontent.com/pod-product-compliance
Lightning Source LLC
Chambersburg PA
CBHW081119180526
45170CB00008B/2916